DEBORAH BOYLAND

FinTech Marketing: Zero to Unicorn in 10 Easy Steps

Copyright © 2022 by Deborah Boyland

All rights reserved. No part of this publication may be reproduced, stored or transmitted in any form or by any means, electronic, mechanical, photocopying, recording, scanning, or otherwise without written permission from the publisher. It is illegal to copy this book, post it to a website, or distribute it by any other means without permission.

This novel is entirely a work of fiction. The names, characters and incidents portrayed in it are the work of the author's imagination. Any resemblance to actual persons, living or dead, events or localities is entirely coincidental.

Deborah Boyland has no responsibility for the persistence or accuracy of URLs for external or third-party Internet Websites referred to in this publication and does not guarantee that any content on such Websites is, or will remain, accurate or appropriate.

Designations used by companies to distinguish their products are often claimed as trademarks. All brand names and product names used in this book and on its cover are trade names, service marks, trademarks and registered trademarks of their respective owners. The publishers and the book are not associated with any product or vendor mentioned in this book. None of the companies referenced within the book have endorsed the book.

First edition

ISBN: 9798355368456

*This book was professionally typeset on Reedsy.
Find out more at reedsy.com*

Contents

Introduction	1
Strategy	3
Building Trust	3
Are You B2B or B2C, And What Does That Mean For Your Business?	7
Find Your Tribe	15
Content	18
Articles	20
Video	25
Podcasts	28
Website	33
The Basic Anatomy of a Landing Page	33
Where to Build Your FinTech Website	40
Enhancing Your Visitors' Customer Experience	43
Boosting Your Website's CRO	44
Search Engines	47
Search Engine Optimization	48
Search Engine Marketing	53
Step-by-Step: How to Use Google Ads	57
Organic Social	61
Start Building Your Social Media Presence in 3 Steps	61
The Growing Importance of Thought Leadership on Social Media	67
The 5 Key Social Media Platforms & How to Use Them	68
Paid Social	76
The Five Layers of Paid Social	77
Creating Meta Ads	80

LinkedIn Advertising	84
TikTok Advertising	86
Best Practices for Effective Social Media Ad Campaigns	88
Events	89
The Value of Experiential Marketing	89
The Anatomy of a Successful Event	90
How to Plan an Event Budget	92
Coordinating a Small Event	94
Coordinating a Large Event	97
Creating an Online Event	99
Influencer Marketing	101
Top FinTech Influencers	101
How to Work with Influencers	103
How to Build Your Own Audience on LinkedIn	106
Press	109
The Importance of Positive Media Attention	109
FinTech Companies & Bad PR: A Cautionary Tale	111
The Role of Guerilla Marketing in FinTech	113
How to Get Good Press: 5 Steps for Attracting Positive Media Attention	114
How to Know When You Have a Sellable Story	119
Newsletters	121
Why Start a Newsletter?	121
How to Start a Newsletter	123
Thank You	134
References	135

To Ilyas and AJ...

And the creators of Witcher 3

Thank you for the endless hours of entertainment

Introduction

This book is meant for founders, business leaders, and new marketing people joining (or hoping to join) the exciting world of FinTech marketing. If you're a CMO, you likely already know many of this book's concepts.

My introduction to financial markets came at a very young age. Growing up, my dad was the Chief Technology Officer at JP Morgan. As a result, I've had a very different experience with banks and their financial markets colleagues compared to the general population. I've been given a unique insight into what drives the banking world and the people behind it.

Films like the *Big Short* and *Wolf of Wall Street* focus on a tiny portion of the banking world. Most people in banking are very kind, insightful people with a genuine interest in positively impacting the planet. It's just that their version of a positive result is different from that of an 18-year-old university students. They see that commerce, trade, and employment are the solutions to increasing the standard of life for many across the globe.

Who's right is a question for an economist or philosopher. This is a marketing book. And if you're a FinTech, these may be the people you're going to market to. They could also be your competitors, your investors, or maybe you're even one of them.

Yes, they can be challenging. Sometimes, they can talk in so much jargon they make your head spin. However, that's true of many industries.

My introduction to marketing came a little later. At 16, I was putting together decks for a company in Brazil. I wasn't sure what I was doing, and I'm almost positive none of them were used. Later, I created websites and wrote website content in NYC. Finally, I landed in a small SaaS company servicing the events industry in London.

As it was a small company, I had to figure out everything independently. This experience, and freedom, proved invaluable to my career. Most marketing people specialize in one area. I learned about them. I was the writer, the website developer, the social media manager, the email marketer, and everything in between.

As the company worked in the events industry and serviced event agencies, I also gained a strong understanding of events and how agencies put them together. This has given me if anything, an appreciation for event agencies and a strong compassion for the prices they charge. Of all marketers, I believe event producers are the ones who wake up first and go to bed last.

I then moved back into FinTech and the financial markets, eventually becoming Head of Marketing at a FinTech company that operates across the Americas. They market to Tier 1 banks, insurance companies, and financial services businesses in three languages.

Now we arrive today. Alongside my role as Head of Marketing, I am now the founder of a FinTech content marketing agency called FinTech Content Ltd, which operates globally out of London. My agency works exclusively with FinTechs and financial markets businesses. I live and breathe FinTech and marketing. And I'm going to tell you in this straightforward step-by-step guide how to get your name out there and make a lot of noise for your FinTech by using digital marketing.

A note: I mention a few tools/products repeatedly. No one is paying me for these mentions. Any product included in this book has been added because I think they have value.

Strategy

"Early-stage FinTech startups often start from excessive top-down hiring and excessive product and feature roadmap. Nail down your first use cases, sharpen up your ICP validation, and go out there and sell. You need 3 people to execute that, and none of them have to be C-level."

- Anna Herman, Founder at Performance Marketing B2B

Building Trust

The most important thing to realize about marketing as a FinTech is that your job is to build trust. Whether marketing your technology services to Tier 1 banks or your neobank to Gen Z, FinTech marketing is all about trust.

I'd go further and say the financial markets as an industry is built on trust. Money is a social construct; we're all just trusting each other to keep believing in it. Well, marketing goes a step further; it says don't just believe in money, believe in me to touch, be near, or manage your money. As a technology company, I promise my technology won't fail or crash and lose all your money.

So, how do you build trust?

At a house party in my younger, stupider days, I became very close friends with someone within the first thirty minutes. We realized early on how much we had in common and knew we would be fast friends.

As the hours started dragging on and the evening turned to night, my new friend started making more requests of me. Can I borrow this? Sure. Can I have your drink? No problem. Can I have your next drink? Okay. Give me a few of your cigarettes. Sure.

Within a few hours, young-broke-student-Deborah was out of cigarettes, food, and alcohol. Which was fine; there was a shop nearby. I asked my new best friend to walk with me to the shop, it was a summer evening, and the crisp air would be nice. He refused; he was enjoying the vibe of the house and didn't want to leave.

Okay, no problem. One of my older friends came with me. I paid for my new alcohol, cigarettes, and food, and we returned to the house. As soon as I entered, my new friend joined me, and it began again. This continued into the early hours of the morning. As my drinks depleted with startling speed, I started to lose interest in my friend.

He was the same person, the conversation was still great, and we had a lot in common, but the feeling had dried out. By the time I had four cigarettes left in my third pack of the night, I had grown tired of this game. The next time he asked, I said no. He seemed to realize he'd made a mistake and started trying to back-peddle, but it was too late.

What did that guy do wrong?

At first, it might feel like the dissolution of our friendship occurred because he asked for too much. That's not the case; I've shared twice as much with other friends without batting an eyelid. People like to share, and they want to trust. It's nice to feel depended on.

No, his issue was two-fold. The first is that he moved too fast. He didn't build a rapport. Friendships aren't made in half an hour, one night, or one interaction. They're built over time.

The second is that he didn't contribute enough to the relationship. Contributing doesn't have to be a financial contribution. If he'd escorted me to the shop, offered to make me some food when we were hungry, or taught me something valuable during our conversation, I likely wouldn't have noticed my depleting resources.

Don't be like that guy. If you want to build trust, which you should, make sure your marketing does two things:

1. Moves at a steady pace, with multiple interactions before getting to the ask
2. Provides value, not just as a product or service, but as a marketing channel

Multiple Touch Points

Let's take my agency as an example. This book is an example of content marketing. I own a FinTech marketing agency called FinTech Content Ltd, so writing this book is a great way to market my agency.

Do I expect strangers who have never heard of me to read this book, then immediately send me an email requesting my agency's services? No. The actual point of this book from a marketing perspective looks more like this:

1. Potential client finds and reads my book
2. Person goes on my LinkedIn to see what I'm doing now and connects with me
3. Person forgets about me
4. I post both articles and social posts regularly to my LinkedIn; they see them over time and feel closer to me as a person
5. One day, they see a post they resonate with, they reach out, I send them my costs, and they think about soliciting my services
6. Person forgets me
7. When they reached out because they went on my website and put their name and email address, they get automatically inserted into a system that retargets them on social media
8. They see my ads on Instagram ads and Facebook. However, I've set up my ads to ensure a certain period lapses between each ad to ensure my potential client doesn't get irritated by seeing the same ad repeatedly. When the potential clients see my ad, they're reminded of how much they liked my book and my branding content on LinkedIn and decided they'd like to use my services.
9. Client signs up

10. Client is added to a newsletter list that provides sporadic, valuable content with the option to personalize the frequency of the letters. It's important to note that marketing is not just about attraction but also retaining customers.

As you can see, multiple touch points don't just help attract clients; they help create happy, long-term clients too. By interacting with your content or social media often before signing up, clients understand what you do and where the value lies, and they know how you work. This leads to fewer surprises and a happier long-term customer.

Providing Value

When it comes to providing value, I've been hard-pressed to find a marketing team that does this better than HubSpot. HubSpot plays the long game, and they start years in advance.

Thinking of getting a job in marketing but don't know where to start? Get a free, industry-relevant, certified course on HubSpot. Want to hear the latest inbound marketing tactics with real-life examples? HubSpot has the answer. Want to increase your expertise in social media? HubSpot. Are you wondering how to train your marketing team cost-effectively? Get them to take HubSpot courses.

By the time you're a grown-up, senior marketing leader with buying power, you're grateful to give back to HubSpot finally. You're almost salivating at the chance to be a part of the HubSpot crew. One of the most significant failures of my career is that I wasn't successfully promoting HubSpot internally when one of my employers was looking for a new CRM, and I promise you, I pushed hard.

Pick one specific area you want to be known for, then produce so much value in that area that your clients become desperate to pay you back. For example, if you're marketing a young micro-investing tool, you could create a series of courses that teaches young investors how to choose their investments.

The first, or beginner's course, could start with the benefits of index funds.

The intermediate course could look at bitcoin and how to distinguish which direction a coin is heading in. The expert course could teach young investors how to look into the background and finances of a company they may want to invest in and provide valuable resources to help them in their search.

By teaching and guiding your target audience, you become a valuable part of their journey, and it'll be a no-brainer which app they sign up with when they're finally ready to make the plunge.

Are You B2B or B2C, And What Does That Mean For Your Business?

B2B

B2B stands for business to business. B2B businesses service or sell to other companies. The people B2B marketers are selling to buy things on their company's behalf. B2B companies include Funding Circle, Finastra, and Tide.

B2C

B2C stands for business to consumer. B2C companies focus on the individual consumer. Their marketing, products, and services are focused on the end user. B2C companies include Klarna, ClearScore, and Monzo.

Mixing it up

Many businesses fit into both. This can make their marketing a little more complicated. The use of multiple social media accounts targeting different demographics and clever paid social are some of the techniques these businesses use to manage this. Another strategy can include focusing on your B2C marketing and driving a strong brand presence that attracts B2B clients without directly marketing to them. Some examples of companies who service both include Starling Bank, Transferwise, and Revolut.

Why Should You Care About the Difference?

While there are many similarities between them, successful marketing as a FinTech depends on you understanding your target audience and buyer. This understanding can help you gain insight into the motivations behind your target market.

Think of the purchases you make in your everyday life, the things you buy for yourself or your family. Then, consider purchases you make on behalf of your business. Think about the motivations behind your purchases on both occasions. Often, we purchase things for one of several reasons:

- The item will make our life easier
- We think it will make us look better in the eyes of others
- It solves a problem we're facing
- It helps us achieve our personal goals
- It will improve our lives in the long run
- It makes us feel like we're a part of something bigger than ourselves
- It gives us a way into a community we would like access to

These motivations are true for B2B and B2C purchases, but the environments in which these motivations occur are different. Let's take apart two separate purchase and look at the motivations behind them.

Scenario A: Katie wants to make her family happy by getting a new promotion. A new promotion would mean more money, more security, and more pride from her partner and children. Katie thinks her promotion will make other people see her as more valuable. Katie walks into a clothing store. She sees a beautiful, successful-looking model up behind the counter. The model is a conference room, and she's leading the group. The model is wearing an outfit with a very bold print. Everyone else is wearing black. The model stands out, and she's been rewarded for it by taking the seat at the top of the table. Katie buys the bold print rather than the black one hoping it will help her stand out at work and take her one step closer to the promotion and the respect of her family.

Scenario B: Katie is at work. She still wants a promotion. Her reasons for wanting a promotion are the same, but now she's at work surrounded by her work colleagues. Katie has a big project coming up, and she has to decide between two consulting firms to help her. One is a thirty-year-old firm that charges a fortune but has a strong name in the field. The other is an exciting challenger firm that charges half the price. It's only been around for two years, but it's an impeccable track record. The track record of the older firm, when you look into it, is not actually that great. The older firm uses lots of indigo blue in their presentations and images of people working in offices dressed smartly. The younger firm uses fresh pastel colors and more funky graphic designs. Katie goes for the older firm.

Her motivations behind each purchase were the same, and so were the branding decisions of each company. Deeper than the promotion is her inspiration to make her family happy, provide for her loved ones and feel the respect of their confidence in her decisions. However, her decision for each was different. With the B2C purchase, she went for the choice that felt bolder. With the B2B purchase, she went for the safe-seeming one, despite its poorer track record and more expensive price tag. Katie was willing to bet on a riskier outfit choice but not on an up-and-coming business.

Despite playing on a similar need, the marketing team of each company would be better off going for different branding. Understand who you're selling to, and you're already halfway to great marketing.

The similarities

While there are several differences between B2B and B2C marketing, they can learn much from each other. Traditionally, in financial markets, B2B businesses will dismiss many of the most successful forms of marketing by assuming they're only for B2C marketers. A great example of this is influencer marketing.

Influencer Marketing

Influencer marketing has taken the B2C world by storm. But financial markets, both B2B and B2C, have been slow to adopt this form of marketing and in some circles, are quick to belittle it.

B2B businesses have been even quicker to dismiss influencer marketing. However, influencer marketing actually fits in very well with the financial markets' business to business way of doing things. Who you know, and what they think of you has a big impact in the financial services industry. While the right friends aren't everything, they do get you in the room.

When Covid-19 hit, there were no more rooms to get into. Everything went digital. Influencer marketing is a way to take the B2B FinTech way of doing things, put it on a digital platform, and scale it. Now, who you know could be in the open for everyone to see.

When I was 16 and eavesdropping, I remember hearing bankers talking about the powerful effect of LinkedIn. I thought it sounded like Facebook but for older adults. I was wrong. Facebook is now Facebook for older adults, and LinkedIn is your key to the business world, even if you have social anxiety.

Don't know how to talk to people? Don't like going outside? No problem, you can connect and network with financial services businesses worldwide from your living room, and influencer marketing is the way to do that.

In a later chapter, we'll discuss the specific benefits of influencer marketing and how to start a campaign. For now, the bottom line is, like 16-year-olds on TikTok, business people often trust the people they look up to in the industry more than they trust an advert that pops up on their social media.

Build Relationships with Your Marketing Funnel

Another place B2B and B2C intersect is that they should both be using marketing to build relationships with their buyers. There are multiple touchpoints to your marketing. This is usually called the marketing funnel and varies from business to business. I'll go into the funnel in more detail later. The general view is that the funnel starts with awareness, goes on to interest, then into consideration, and finally on to conversion. I think there should be an additional layer after that, retention. Think of your marketing funnel as a formal way to make a friend. To first make a friend, they have to meet you. This usually happens in the open, at a party, or through another friend.

This is your awareness level, and it's just getting your name out there. Good ways of getting your name out there include creating educational content that is of interest to your audience, then distributing that content through various paid and organic channels, anywhere your audience is. The content should not talk too much about your product or service.

The next layer is interest. This is where you're getting to know each other. For both B2B and B2C, the interest layer includes more detailed content that introduces what you're offering.

Potential buyers then move on to consideration. Consideration includes case studies, offers, price comparisons and free trials. While case studies will look very different for B2B vs. B2C, there should be careful attention from both sides. B2C should aim to get reviews both on their own channels and externally in video and written format; B2B should work on building out official case studies their potential clients can review when making a decision.

After that comes conversion, the conversion layer is really just about getting out of the way of your customer purchasing. For B2C, the conversion marketing can include tactics like shopping cart abandonment follow-ups or ensuring that purchases are a seamless experience. For example, let's say someone gets halfway to signing up for your online digital bank, but maybe an annoying pop-up won't go away at that moment. They try to click backspace, but instead of removing the pop-up, it sends them back to a previous page where they have to re-enter all of their details. They think this isn't worth it and decide not to sign up. We've all experienced website issues like this, be sure to check that your purchasing experience is seamless.

While the rest of the funnel looks very similar, the conversion layer differs significantly between enterprise B2B and small-ticket B2B or B2C. This is because often, with enterprise B2B purchases, if you're selling something that costs a lot of money, it might be done with the sales team, and procurement might get involved. Consider all the players involved in pushing through a deal, and then think about which one's it's financial beneficial to target with your marketing.

One small comment is that if you are a B2B company that sells something under the £200 mark, it can sometimes benefit you from a marketing perspective to act like a B2C company.

Lastly, there's retention. Retention is often ignored, but it should be just as crucial to the marketing team as it is to the account management team. Retention marketing is just trying to make your buyer feel like they're part of a community after they've purchased. This can be done through several means. For example, you could invite them to exclusive events. These are very useful; as if the events are valuable to your buyers in and of themselves, they can become part of the reason for working with you. Another way to create a buyer community is to send out buyer-specific newsletters. If you use this tactic, remove all buyers from your prospect newsletter to ensure they aren't overwhelmed with emails. Another technique is to create a private Facebook group, Slack, or LinkedIn group for post-purchase. Fill it with fun videos, let buyers talk to and help each other, answer the questions any of your buyers have and post unique, helpful content that helps improve their experience once they've purchased. Occasionally, you can also use this group to upsell to a community of people who already know and like your brand.

The timing of these layers can move quickly or slowly, depending on the situation. For example, Experian recently launched an advertisement in the UK. The advert grabbed its audience's attention by showing a man in a dentist's chair about to launch into space. It then moved the audience into interest within the same advert by saying you could immediately increase your credit score. You could then sign up for an account and start using Experian® Boost for free, making the consideration stage easy to access. Within the site, after signing up, you could purchase a monthly subscription to Experian CreditExpert®, which would help you build your credit score further and protect yourself from fraud. Experian then helped retain their customers by providing a great product that helped them develop their finances for their future life.

It generally takes 3 – 6 touches for you to convert someone into a client, so however long your funnel is, ensure you're not just showing adverts once to your prospects and then stopping. The real magic happens when you retarget.

Connect on an emotional level

Business buyers are people too. Whether you're working on content marketing or social media, remembering to connect on a personal level with both B2B and B2C buyers. What are your buyers motivations behind purchasing your product? Music, nostalgia, and shared experiences are great ways to connect to your buyer emotionally.

The differences

The differences between B2B and B2C marketing are far fewer than expected. Many successful B2B businesses get their marketing strategies from copying B2C campaigns. However, here are some.

Time

The main difference is time. Marketers are always talking about people's short attention spans, and it's true; the faster you can make the delivery of your information, the better. However, it's also true that much of marketing happens where we find our entertainment; our phones, the television, and social media.

We have infinitely more time for these things, particularly for anything that is genuinely entertaining and takes place on a medium we feel comfortable with. While delivering B2C FinTech products to the consumer market, as long as you make your marketing fun or educational and, most importantly, simple, you can take up much more time than marketers traditionally suggest.

The timing is different for B2B. B2B people are often at work or hearing about work outside of working hours. They may be about to go into a meeting or trying to spend time with their family. Be careful of how you time your campaigns; for example, you might prefer to narrow the timing of a Google ads campaign to working hours if you're targeting a junior person, as they may have been allotted a certain period to research new tools. Consider when and how your target audience looks for the information you're providing.

Price

The lifecycle and the actual cost of advertising can be more expensive when marketing B2B. Fun, exciting tools such as TikTok provide advertising options for smaller budgets and are great for B2C companies testing the waters. B2B companies testing the waters have fewer, much more expensive options.

You may also face multiple touch points; for example, procurement, finance, and senior leadership may all have a say in purchasing your tool or service. In B2C, you usually target and sell to one person. They may ask their partner or family, but that's less of a block than an entire department having to sign off on something.

The pricing is also affected by the timing. If you're launching a B2C product, you might use TikTok to test the advertising waters. You could put in £100, and if you don't make £300, you have accurate data to help you decide on your marketing spend strategy. On the other hand, if you're a B2B company, you could spend £20,000 on advertising, but the purchase lifecycle might take up to 6 months, so you're waiting much longer to get the return on your investment, and your insights into the market are slower.

A Note: Don't make the mistake of thinking that exclusively targeting CEOs will help you lower your marketing costs if you're B2B. CEOs often have less of a reason to buy something than their team. They may forward an ad or email to the appropriate person, but no one wants to feel like their CEO is shoving a product down their throat. CEOs are very busy, very expensive to market to, and do not just tell their teams what to purchase. They are leaders, and their job is to lead, not to decide which CRM tool to use.

Find Your Tribe

Finding the right people is the first step to capturing their attention and converting your target demographic into loyal, paying customers.

Identify your Target Demographic

Your target demographic is the people for whom you are solving a problem. Here are some questions to ask about your audience that will help define this for your:

- What's their big pain point?
- What solutions have they tried so far, and why didn't those solutions work?
- What does your target person do in the morning? Do they head straight for the TV, check their emails, scroll through LinkedIn, or post a TikTok?
- What do they do before bed? Do they check Facebook or look at Instagram?
- What are their favorite brands? What do they like about those brands?
- What drives them? Are they driven by their family, wealth? Maybe they want to move country, or want to get married. How can you help them feel closer to those goals?
- Where do they go when they have a question? Reddit, Facebook groups, or do they read articles? If they read articles for information, which media channels do they use?
- Where are they in the world right now?

The answers to these questions will help you define your target market. For example, if your target person wakes up at 5 am and checks their Instagram stories, you should be posting Instagram stories at 4:30 am every day. If your persona (or ideal customer) is about 50 years old, has a house worth £500,000, and a job that pays $50,000 a year, you now have the demographics you should target in your paid social ad campaigns on Facebook.

Ask Questions

Use the analytics you already have available to you to define your audience further, but also, don't forget to ask your customers for the answers you need. Who currently buys from you? How did they find you? What do they like about you? What don't they like? Your current customers should impact how you market in the future.

Research Agencies

Research companies can sometimes provide the answers to many of your questions through various means. One of the most common ways of sourcing answers is by performing surveys either digitally or over the phone. Depending on the agency, the people they survey could be senior executives they already know, or they could be cold calling a list of people that might fit your target market.

Costs vary. The prices I've come across range from $4000 for a one-off project where they provide the answers to ten of your most pressing questions up to $100,000 a year for access to their research library.

Research agencies can provide a great way to get a unique insight into your buyer persona. Many are familiar with buyer personas and work closely with marketing teams. Others specialize in FinTech and in more drilled-down areas, such as payments or retail banking. They can often help you build out your persona as well as help you understand what your audience is looking for from both a product and marketing perspective.

Another benefit many research agencies offer is the ability to double up the research they do for you as unique insights to include in your content. Using the analysis you've commissioned as content can be a powerful tool in your marketing, particularly for B2B FinTechs – think "a survey conducted by."

When displaying your research, you might like to put it together as an infographic. Infographics can be commissioned from freelancers on popular platforms like Fiverr or Upwork, or the research agency might offer it as a side product on occasion. You could try your hand at Canva. Watch a few videos to get to grips with how to use Canva, type infographics into the Canva templates, and make sure to use your brand colors, fonts, and logos.

Content

"I could not more strongly believe in content marketing. It is the hymn sheet for your community to galvanise them around a topic, belief system or way of thinking but scaled for a digital age distributed through social media platforms. If you're a b2b business it is golf and coffees for this generation, if you're a b2c its the way to turn your product into a community movement. Any which way you look at it today every single business is a content business manifesting your brand to potential customers and employees. The more value you create for your consumers through your content the more value your content will create for your business in return."

- David M. Brear, CEO of 11:FS and LinkedIn Top Voice

You would honestly be shocked how often I see companies produce a load of content, or commission a bunch of articles, or create a great big strategy, and then that content never sees the light of day. This happens for several reasons:

- Perfectionism
- Leadership in-fighting
- Not finding a good writer
- No one feeling empowered enough to decide content can go live
- No one properly understanding how to post content to the website

Here's the thing. Content isn't about one, perfect article. It's about a consistent stream of strategic valuable written, visual, or audio content designed to attract and retain a relevant audience.

The first article you publish isn't going to be perfect, neither is the first video, or the first podcast. And that's okay. It doesn't have to be, it just has to be relevant, insightful, valuable, and targeted.

If you never post content, you're missing out on so much. You're missing out on leads, traffic, and an audience that listens to you. But the most important thing you're missing out on, are lessons.

When you publish regular, consistent content, you learn something. You learn what your audience is interested in, you learn what they're not interested in, you learn what format of content engages them best, and you learn which forms of content have the best impact on SEO. With that learning, comes growth.

Start posting, and start today. Not tomorrow, and definitely not once every executive and their mother, sister, and cousins, have read through the content and changed it until it's lacking all personality and sounds like a corporate manifesto.

Not only is content a great marketing tool in and of itself, it also provides the backbone to a lot of other marketing channels. Once you have a steady stream of articles, you have content to repurpose for paid social, organic social, influencer marketing and more.

Some common examples of content marketing include:

- Blogs
- Articles
- Whitepapers
- Videos
- Interactive Media
- Podcasts

Evergreen or Topical?

Content is either evergreen or topical, and both have their place. Evergreen is content that still gathers leads and interested readers as the years go on. It's content that is relevant and interesting long after it's written. Topical content is relevant right now. It usually relates to a trend, event, or exciting news topic. It has a much shorter marketing lifespan but should still hold a firm place in your monthly content strategy.

A typical example of evergreen content is blog articles. Anything that provides guidance that stands the test of time or provides insight into something useful is evergreen. Your content strategy should include a lot of evergreen content. It's also important to note that a good SEO strategy includes regularly updating evergreen content.

Articles

Let's start with the holy grail of content marketing; blogs and articles. Consistent articles published to a relevant section of your website give you credibility as a company and authority. They increase your visibility, and help ensure you're taken seriously by prospects.

They're also time-consuming. In fact, when I first became Head of Marketing at a Financial Services business, they were the most time-consuming part of my job. Finding a writer who fit my budget and worked hard to hard to understand what we did honestly saved my life.

To publish regular content, you've got a few options:

- Write the articles yourself
- Allocate them to someone in your team
- Hire a writer internally
- Hire a contractor or micro-agency
- Hire an agency

So which should you do?

Writing articles yourself

This might feel like the least expensive, but often isn't. Like with many outsourcing decisions, I like to consider how much time my personal time is worth, and then see if I can find someone who charges less than that. For example, let's say my hourly rate is £30, and it takes me four hours to write an article, that makes the cost of an article I write myself £120. So if I can find a writer who charges £100 per article, I've saved myself £20.

There are also expertise costs. Writing articles myself means I have to learn how to write the articles in a way that best attracts my audience, if I can find a writer who already understands industry best practices, can learn my sector, and knows how to write a genuinely engaging piece, I'm saving myself the potential revenue I'd lose while I learnt all that on my own.

However, as my mum always told me, if you don't understand how to do something, hiring someone to take it over will always end with problems. So doing some research into content marketing before offloading to someone else is always best.

Allocate them to someone in your team

If the person you're allocating them to is a writer, this is a great idea. If they're not, you run the risk of creating discontent. If you do allocate content marketing to someone in your team, be sure to recognize how much time articles really take. Getting into the right headspace, thinking about the article, giving it space to breathe before editing, and research should all be considered when deciding if someone has the time and space to do a good job at content marketing.

One thing I've seen a lot of businesses do is hiring a single marketing person to run, strategize and execute the entire marketing department alone. This is usually done due to budget constraints, but can lead to a very stressed-out team member.

If this is the case at your business, understand that content marketing is a beast of it's own, and giving your overrun marketing person some regular content will honestly be a lifesaver for them.

Hire a writer internally

If hiring a writer internally is within your budget, it's a great option. They're able to learn how your business works, grow with your team, and they can help write other content like the content you post to social media, personal branding content for your execs, or invites to events.

When looking for a writer to onboard internally, focus more on their writing skills and attitude, as opposed to their experience in your sector. They're going to be with you for a while, so there'll be lots to learn anyway, and it makes sense to invest that extra time in helping them get familiar with your industry.

Hire a contractor or micro-agency

Micro-agencies are small, mini agencies made up of under 5 people. Since they function similarly to contractors, we'll group them together for this one.

Contractors come in many shapes and sizes. The benefit of hiring one is that you can usually find someone who specializes in your field. While any writer needs a month or two to really get to grips with the kind of content you need, the right contractor or micro-agency can reduce this time down a lot.

When looking for a contractor or micro-agency, unlike an internal writer, I would definitely look for someone who has industry experience, as well as a reasonable amount of samples in your sector.

Also, ask your contractor if they have any understanding of SEO best practices, or if they have any experience in putting together a content strategy, as you may be able to save your team some time and stress by having a contractor who can do more than execute a content marketing plan.

Hire an agency

Depending on the agency, this is usually the most expensive of the options. It can also be the least demanding on your time, as many agencies offer content strategies as part of their packages. Some even offer website upload, pre-written metadata, and social media posting along with their content packages. If your chosen agency doesn't usually provide these, ask anyway, as they may include them for free if prompted.

When looking for an agency, make sure to get a reasonable understanding of who will actually be writing your pieces, and if they have any experience in your sector.

Putting together a brief

If you're planning to send briefs, here's what you should include in a brief:

- The SEO keywords you want to target
- The person your article is targeting
- The point of the article and it's position in the marketing funnel
- The suggested headline (request additional headlines to choose from if appropriate)
- A brief description and outline
- Articles you like that are relevant to this article

How much should you pay?

If you're hiring a contractor or agency, I've seen everything between £200 a month and £18,000 a month for 4 – 8 articles a month on an ongoing basis. Agencies often caution against paying by wordcount, and while it's true wordcount has its faults, it can give smaller marketing teams some flexibility and a bit of space to experiment.

Another way to pay is by retainer. If you're working with freelancers, a retainer can be a good way to give them some security, making them more loyal to your business. Some agencies charge by page. This is similar to wordcount at its core, but can lead to issues if your SEO team needs a "page" to be in teeny tiny font and come out to 2000 words but your agency wants to give you a "page" that's written in normal font and comes out to 600 words. Others charge by time, which can be ineffective, as you're paying for work rather than results.

The most common way of charging is by project, or piece, and it's most common for a reason. By project is a great way to ensure you're paying as much as you expected, you know the costs upfront, and the writer gets a good understanding of what they're getting each month or quarter. Make sure you outline what the project entails, how much detail is expected for each section and how many revisions will be provided if you're not happy with the end product.

Revisions are normal, so please don't be shy when sending them, your freelancer or agency is likely used to them.

Word Count

How many words is too many? The answer to this lies in your content goals. From a readability perspective, regardless of whether the company is B2B or B2C, 500-700 word articles are easier to digest. Anything over 2000 words would fare better in eBook or whitepaper format. The most important aspect for readability and building a long-term audience is whether or not your content is enjoyable. The best advice I can give on word count is use as many words as you need to say what you would like to say without rambling. Be concise, create a structure before you start, and try to cut out anything unnecessary when you edit.

On the other hand, when looking at wordcount from an SEO perspective, every marketer and agency will have a different answer. From my personal experiments and experience, 2000 word articles still have huge ranking potential, although I know many disagree with me. If you're using content for SEO, I've personally found a strategy that mixes up long form and short form content is best. Pick the 5 hardest keywords you'd like to rank for, and write 2000 words on them. Write anything between 700 and 1500 for the rest.

The purpose of search engines is and has always been to bring answers to the public. Their algorithms change in line with this goal. As SEO evolves, it will continue to focus on ranking content that genuinely helps people in a way they can easily digest higher than anything else. While 2000 word articles may rank well today, I personally feel this is because google sees that you've put more effort into these than others. This may change in the future. The best thing you can do for your SEO is the same as the best thing you can do for your readability and brand awareness, focus on driving valuable, easy-to-read, enjoyable content and the rest will follow.

As you look at your marketing funnel, consider that each moment you take from your buyer persona by talking about yourself is like a loan. You are borrowing goodwill from them. At the same time, every moment you give them of enjoyable content is adding more goodwill into your goodwill bucket. Don't waste too much goodwill by writing 5000 word manifestos.

Finally, a word of caution. It is often easier to say more than it is to say less. If you find you are always producing 3000 word articles, it's possible you may need to simplify your marketing.

Video

Create an experience for your buyers by showing them one. Videos can be used in a range of exciting ways, but the most successful one has always been eliciting an emotional response. Reminding your buyers what's important to them will help strengthen customer loyalty and build a brand people remember.

Whether the emotion is courage or nostalgia, connecting your brand with strong emotions is a great marketing technique. Think of an emotion you'd like connected with your brand, then consider an experience your buyer has likely lived through that brought out that emotion, then show them that experience again through the eyes of a camera.

For example, your audience may be mothers between the ages of 35 and

50. The emotion you may like to connect with could be one of love. You could use a video of the first moments after childbirth, or a video of a child on their first day of school waving goodbye. Whatever you choose, truly knowing your audience is the first step to creating a video that will resonate with them.

Film and video have played a strong role in the arts for almost a century now, yet marketers still have a long way to go to take full advantage of these incredible tools. The most common reason for not producing brand videos is time and budget. Overcome these barriers, and you will find a wealth of serious benefits.

How to create videos

The best advice I can give you about video marketing is to get to the point quickly, and subtitle all of your videos.

Like everything in marketing, more time spent, more effort expended, and more of your soul chopped out and fed to the marketing gods does not necessarily mean more success. It's a very strange phenomenon, but the best way I can put it is this; art does not equal sales.

An artistic piece can be great if you're targeting artists or other creative marketers. If you're targeting bankers who just want to know what the hell DevOps is and how they can use it, the artistic parts may just be getting in the way, and you're better off skipping to the point of the thing. Even with large creative agencies, it's often the case that the biggest fans of a video are other creative agencies. But what was really the impact on the paying company's bottom line?

The same thing is true of B2C social media videos. The ones I've produced that were mini episodes the television industry would be proud of flopped. The ones that were filmed in my social media assistant's bedroom with an iPhone succeeded.

You don't need to create something Van Gogh would like.

Video will continue making an impact in the future. A huge amount of people engage with online video because it's often easier to consume than long articles. With improved technology and hosting options, producing video content is no longer the sole territory of production companies. As mentioned, at times, it may be in your best interest to skip elaborate production and instead focus on authentic connection, especially when posting to social media.

When video content is genuine, the trust factor grows. Video content is easier than ever to personalize with software options like Loom, Filmora and DaVinci. Here's how to make a video advert if you want to DIY it:

- Write a script, doesn't have to be long, can be based on an old blog or your current homepage.
- Create a storyboard, just has to be a few pictures of what you'd like each shot to look like, pictures can be found on Pexels.
- Decide who's going to be in the video, will you use a voiceover actor or will you speak yourself? If you're going to speak yourself, record yourself reading out the script. Go slower than you think you should.
- Film your scenes, or use stock video footage, found on sites like ArtGrid or Storyblocks. If you struggle to film your scenes, hire a videographer to film what you're after.
- If you're like me, and you do need a voiceover to read your script out (ever tried to record yourself speaking and hear it back, cringe central), you can find a bunch of really great ones on Fiverr.
- Find some royalty-free music online, this can also be found on Storyblocks. Alternatively, contract a musician to make something unique that fits your brand.
- Most video editors use DaVinci or Adobe, but they are huge products. If it's your first time editing, download Filmora, it's a much simpler, more newbie friendly option. Watch a few YouTube videos to figure out how to piece your videos together, add your voiceover and lay over your music.
- For an extra oomph, add in a small sound at the beginning of each video (these can be found in Filmora) to make it *your* sound. The same way people like to recognise brands through visual themes, adding in a recurring audio theme helps enhance brand recognition.
- Add in the subtitles in Filmora and sync them up to the audio.

- Voila! Upload it to YouTube and your website and you're good to go.

If you'd like to make a social media video, simply record yourself speaking to a camera, then edit the video in Filmora or Instagram. Alternatively, use Loom to record yourself speaking if you'd like to display something on your computer screen at the same time. TikTok is also useful for recording and editing, but TikTok watermark downloads with any videos.

How long should your video be?

Thirty second to two-minute videos are best when you're getting started. That's usually enough time to tell your story and make an impact on your audience.

However, as time goes on, I've found 5 –7 minute videos (and up) to be surprisingly successful. For example, a mini-documentary on an important topic in your industry, that happens to connect to your product, can go on for a much longer period as long as it's gripping.

An example might be a payments company producing a short documentary on the origin and evolution of payments. By not talking about yourself and providing free insights into payments you put yourself in front of your audience in a more open, less intrusive way. In a scenario like this, where you're discussing a more general topic of interest that connects back to your service, longer videos can be suitable.

Podcasts

If you have started to notice an uptick in business-related podcasts, you're not alone.

Industries of all kinds have begun to notice the marketing power of podcasts. From financial advice and technology news shows to investing and early retirement, there's a wide range of podcasts within the FinTech industry alone.

Here's how to start your own.

Setting Up Your Podcast

There are a few essential starter steps to take before recording a podcast, including picking a name and theme.

Your name should be indicative of the type of show you are hosting and the topics you will cover.

A great example of this is the FinTech Insider podcast by 11:FS. "FinTech Insider" has a clear title that conveys what topics are covered while using the powerful keyword "insider" to give listeners a sense of exclusivity.

Once you have your podcast title and theme suggested, your next key tasks include:

- **Putting Together a Questionnaire:** Having a pre-set questionnaire will help you build cohesive episodes with a consistent interview style. However, you should always customize your questions for each specific guest.
- **Building Email & LinkedIn Templates:** Email and LinkedIn are two of the best ways to find and reach out to guests for your show. Building invitation templates for email and LinkedIn to send to your potential guests will save you a lot of time in the long run.
- **Designing a Podcast Cover on Canva:** For many podcast listeners, a well-designed podcast cover can be what initially draws them in.

Finding & Interviewing Guests on Your Podcast

Most podcasts will have a central theme that all episodes revolve around, such as financial education. After choosing your theme, one of the best ways to make your episodes compelling to listeners is by interviewing experts in the field of your chosen theme.

Here are the 5 key steps to finding and interviewing guests:

1. **Find a Guest and Reach Out to Them:** A good place to start looking for guests is within your own business or company. If you have coworkers who are extremely knowledgeable and passionate about niche FinTech topics, begin by interviewing them about these special interests. This will help build your confidence. From there, move on to finding speakers on LinkedIn or other social media platforms. Look for people in the news who have something topical to share.
2. **Ask Your Guest to Come On Your Show:** When you are just starting a new project, it can feel intimidating to ask others to participate in it, especially when some level of showmanship and charisma is needed. The key is to have confidence in your ideas and convey that confidence to your potential guests. Once you're ready to send out invites, start hitting people up via email or LinkedIn.
3. **Research Your Guest Thoroughly:** Diving into an interview blind is like swimming with the sharks. You not only risk embarrassing yourself but also potentially insulting your guest, who has taken the time out of their busy schedule to be interviewed on your podcast. Always thoroughly research your guests before they come on the show. Before the episode starts, clarify how you pronounce their names and the company's name.
4. **Write Thought-Provoking Questions:** Identity what topics in your theme have already been covered versus those that have been left largely unexplored, and write questions that you feel will bring the best insights out of your guest.
5. **Conduct Your Interview:** Conducting an interview can be nerve-wracking — what's important is to remind yourself that your guest is likely just as, if not more, nervous. Take a deep breath and remember to speak calmly and clearly. Interviews can be recorded easily over a Zoom call. Simply set up the call, click record when you're ready to start, and then click stop when you're finished. Let it render, and edit any sections out using a tool like Filmora, or hire an editor.

Publishing Your Podcast

When your episodes are recorded, edited, and ready for publishing, it's time to choose the best publishing platform for your podcast.

Here are 3 ways you can publish your podcast easily:

1. **Anchor:** Anchor is a free platform for creating, distributing, and monitoring podcasts. This platform is designed to be beginner-friendly and can help you publish a podcast with minimal challenges. Anchor even includes built-in uploading, recording, and editing tools so that you can spend less on equipment and software when starting out. Anchor is what I use.
2. **Spotify or iTunes:** Spotify and iTunes give you access to some of the largest podcast audiences in the world. For both, you will need to submit a podcast through an aggregator (which includes Anchor!).
3. **Website-Hosted:** You could also create your own dedicated website and upload your podcast directly to this site. This can be a good option if you have a bigger team, but may lack the tools and accessibility of an established platform.

Growing an Audience for Your Podcast

Your final step is to grow your audience. There are many ways to grow your podcast, both organically and through paid advertising channels.

Here are some of the best methods for growing an audience for your podcast:

1. **Build a Social Media Presence:** Your social media accounts have a huge role to play in finding your ideal audience and attracting them to your podcast. Sound bytes and entertaining short clips of your podcast can make excellent posts for Instagram, Twitter, and TikTok, helping to build a transferable audience across all your platforms.
2. **Advertise on Similar Podcasts:** One of the best ways to reach your ideal audience is to go to them directly. Reach out to the hosts of similar

podcasts, and see if they'd be open to letting you advertise your podcast.
3. **Encourage Likes, Comments, & Shares:** Encourage your listeners to regularly like, comment on, and share your podcast episodes. You can motivate listeners even more by doing special shoutouts during your show for listeners who leave a comment on your latest episodes.

Like any project, you will have both successes and failures in your podcasting journey.

The key is to always welcome feedback from guests and listeners alike, making changes as needed. Unless you are a podcast protégé, you are bound to make a mistake or two along the way, I know I did — just pay attention to where you are thriving versus which areas of your podcast may need some extra care.

Website

"When the services you're offering are complicated, do your best to explain them in a simple way on every single web page. Of course, it's essential to follow best practices for SEO content, but at the end of the day, your audience is human, and nobody wants to have to guess what you're selling."

- Julian Tavalin, Director of Content Marketing, Exadel

Your website should serve as a cornerstone to your brand, representing a guiding post that your customers can always return to for help.

The Basic Anatomy of a Landing Page

As you build your FinTech company website, the very first element you need to focus on is creating an effective home landing page.

A **landing page** is — in simple terms — the webpage a visitor lands on when they type in a web address or click a link found on an ad or search engine. Your home landing page is like the cover of a book, helping to paint your brand clearly and provide customers with a guiding story focused on their needs.

The 5 most important elements of an effective landing page are:

1. The Header

2. The Introduction
3. The Value Proposition
4. The Risks & Rewards
5. The How-To Section

1. The Header

The header of your website is the information found at the very top of the page to the bottom of the screen before scrolling. In this header, there are several key pieces of information to include, such as:

- **Your Company Name:** As you build your website, you should keep in mind how consistent your website branding is with the rest of your marketing materials. Along with listing your company name — either large and in the center or smaller in the top right corner — you should also match the font and colour to match your existing branding and logo.
- **A Tagline or Headline:** A website tagline (also called a headline) is a concise statement displayed at the top of your webpage that describes who you are, what you do, and what customers can expect from you. Some companies will choose to include a paragraph below their tagline to further explain the company, but the tagline itself should ideally be less than 10 words.
- **A Website Menu:** If your website has more than one webpage, you will need an easy-to-find menu located in your header. You can choose from many different styles of menus, it just needs to be recognizable as a menu to the average web user. Menus are typically placed in the upper right-hand corner of a website.

Your first **call to action** (CTA) should be found in the header of your website as well, typically placed directly below your tagline. This CTA should encourage the visitor to take the most important action, whether that's signing up for a service online or scheduling a consultation.

To write a CTA, make sure to include:

- **A Strong Command Verb:** A command verb is a type of action verb used to get a person to do what you want them to do. Strong examples of command verbs include "join", "call", and "start". The verb you choose should also accurately suggest what action the CTA button leads to, such as a sign-up form or contact page.
- **Short Sentence Structure:** In terms of how long your CTA should be, the general rule of thumb is to stick to 25 characters or less (including spaces). For instance, your CTA could be as short as "Join Now" or as long as "Join Today and Save More".
- **Emotional Value:** Try to inject some emotional impact into your CTAs. For example, you might include looming regulatory deadlines, or a time-sensitive offer.

2. The Introduction

Following your header is your introductory paragraph where you would provide a more in-depth, but still concise, explanation of your company.

This introduction can be located either directly below your header tagline or further down the page as the first item that appears when a visitor scrolls. In general, I recommend keeping it above the fold and making it visible before the visitor needs to scroll.

With each new section of your website, you want the customer to feel as though they are naturally progressing through a story and having their questions answered before they even think of them.

Here's an example of a weak introductory paragraph:

"Welcome to ABC FinTech Services, your place for all things FinTech. At ABC, we are committed to a high level of client satisfaction and always make sure our customers have their specific needs met. Don't hesitate to give us a call about our many services."

What's wrong with this example?

The main issue with this introductory paragraph is that it's too vague. Chances are that if a visitor has arrived at your website, they are already on the hunt for FinTech services. Instead, this introduction should focus on the specific services offered by the company and how the customer can benefit from them.

Here's a stronger version of this introduction:

"At ABC FinTech Services, we are the one-stop shop for payment solutions and platform integrations for eCommerce businesses. From secure online transactions and simple customer refunding processes to 50+ available integrations with other apps and platforms, our team has the capabilities to meet your exact needs. Get a free consultation today."

Why is this example better?

In this corrected example, the introduction includes 3 key pieces of information that make it stronger overall than its predecessor:

1. **Precise Services:** Rather than simply saying they offer FinTech services, this introduction provides a brief explanation of the exact services offered (payment solutions and platform integrations).
2. **Target Industry:** Along with describing the specific services offered, this introduction also states the target industry that the company is trying to attract (eCommerce businesses). Almost all FinTech companies have a target industry or industries and mentioning this in your introduction is a good idea for attracting the right customers.
3. **Exact Numbers:** Since this introduction offers more precise information, it should also list more precise numbers as well. When describing the integrations offered, this introduction states that there are "50+ available integrations with other apps and platforms," letting the customer know right away how powerful the integration service can be.

3. The Value Proposition

Next up we have the value proposition paragraph, which is a segmented explanation of the main benefits of your company's products or services. In this value proposition section of your website, try to outline exactly what your company has to offer and how your services or product can be employed for client use.

Now, you could argue that the entire landing page is a value proposition in and of itself. The key with your value proposition section is to offer a detailed summary that gives the customer all the information they need to know about your products and services in one neat little package.

Your value proposition may include:

- **Key Features and Capabilities:** One of the most important sets of details to include in your value proposition is the main features and capabilities included with your products or services. While you can save super in-depth explanations of how things work for separate product pages, your value proposition should provide a solid overview of what you have to offer.
- **A Hero and a Guide:** Throughout your value proposition, it is important to establish your customer as a hero on a hero's journey and yourself as a guide. In this role of a guide, you place yourself in a position of authority that can guide the hero (your customer) on the correct path towards achieving their goals.
- **Use Cases:** Try to include a few use cases in your value proposition to help demonstrate to viewers how your services can be put to use in real-life scenarios.

This value proposition is the best place to include testimonials and other credentials as well. By providing these in your value proposition, you build greater credibility while also convincing the customer of why they need your products or services.

4. The Risks & Rewards

After you have covered your value proposition, include a risk and rewards section. It is important to have established your customer as the hero on a journey and yourself as the guide before moving into the risks and rewards. This is because the risks in this section refer to the consequences of not utilizing your products or services, while the rewards paint a positive picture for the customer of the results they can achieve with your help.

For example, let's say you run a FinTech company that specializes in digital transformation. Some of the risks you could describe can include:

- **Lack of Competitiveness:** Without your technological expertise, the client will fail to maintain the high level of professional competitiveness needed to remain relevant in their industry.
- **Poor Customer Service:** Without the support of your digital transformation products, the client cannot provide as high-quality customer service as they would hope to.
- **Unnecessary Expenses:** Without your products or services, the client cannot achieve optimal operational efficiency, leading to unnecessary spending.

After you have clearly listed out the risks, you should immediately follow this up with an explanation of the rewards that come with working with your company. These rewards should ideally address the same issues that the risks covered.

In the above example, the rewards may include:

- **Greater Competitive Edge:** With your products and services, your client never has to worry about staying ahead of the competition.
- **Groundbreaking Customer Service:** With your products and services, the client will be better equipped to deal with customer support issues quickly and confidently.
- **Boosted Operational Efficiency:** With your products and services, the client can cut back on operational costs that are hindering their company's overall efficiency.

Remember to keep these risks and rewards brief — these elements of your website are primarily responsible for keeping the visitor interested and leading them into the next section.

5. The How-To Section

The final element on your main landing page should be a how-to section.

This how-to section is where you inform the potential customer of the exact steps they need to take to get started with your company, as well as another CTA button that leads them to your sign-up page.

Ideally, you should keep your how-to section to 5 steps or less — you will only end up losing more leads if your starting process is too long or complicated. Keep things simple and easy to follow, and you will ultimately see greater success in the number of customers your convert through your website.

Here is an example of a how-to section:

Ready to Get Started with ABC FinTech Services? Follow these 3 Key Steps:

1. **Sign-Up:** Enter your email in the form below.
2. **Schedule a Call:** We'll be in touch to schedule a free call with one of our consultants, where we will discuss all of your needs and preferences.
3. **Receive a Custom Solution:** Once we have spoken with you, we will determine a starting quote and custom solution to meet your exact needs. Set up only takes three days, and won't impact your current operations.

In this how-to section, one of the most important factors is mentioning that getting started is free. When you have a free start-up process, you are much more likely to attract a greater number of potential clients. This number will go up further if you offer a free trial or demo period.

Additional Pages to Include on a FinTech Website

Once you have your home landing page squared away, then you should begin considering the additional pages you need to add to your website.

The following four pages are the most important to add to your FinTech website:

- **About Us:** Your "About Us" page is where you will delve into the history and story of your company in greater detail. This may also include a staff directory and company mission statement or values.
- **Product Pages:** If you have more than one product or service, the next step is to create a dedicated web page for each one. Try to mention the features, benefits, and case studies or testimonials for each one.
- **Pricing:** Pricing pages are a bit controversial. Depending on how you price your offerings, this page can vary in degrees of complexity. Wherever you can, I always encourage testing. If you do include a pricing page, include three prices, make the middle price the product you really want to sell, and then feature a cheaper version beside it, and a more expensive one on the other side. This puts website users in a position where they are choosing between three options on your site rather than choosing between working with you or not working with you.
- **Contact:** Always include a content page to help direct potential customers to your preferred channels of communication. This sounds obvious, but make sure the phone number you include has someone answering at the other end. Regularly test all your contact methods.

Where to Build Your FinTech Website

When it comes to choosing where to build your FinTech website, there are seemingly limitless options.

While there are many different platforms and services that allow you to build a website, most can be divided into one of two categories:

1. **Website Building Platforms:** Website building platforms tend to be simpler to use for beginners and include a more intuitive interface. These types of platforms may allow you to edit the coding, but knowledge of coding is not required in most cases.
2. **Content Management Systems:** Content management systems are more

complex platforms that give you a greater level of control over the design and function of your website. However, these systems can have a sharp learning curve for beginners.

Website Building Platforms

Popular website-building platforms include the likes of Wix, Squarespace, and Weebly. On each of these sites, you are given everything you need to easily design your website with drag-and-drop tools and other easy-to-use features.

The main advantages of using a website-building platform include:

- **Simplicity:** If you have little to no experience with web design, then a website-building platform is a good place for you to start. With these platforms, you can play with everything from layout to color theory. Best of all, you do not have to worry about any of the back-end coding, as this is all built-in for your convenience.
- **No Hosting Concerns:** When you run a website through a traditional content management system, you are likely to have to figure out your own web hosting. With a website-building platform, however, the platform acts as the host, eliminating the need for extra spending on a web host.
- **Affordable Domain Names:** With most website building platforms, you can use either a free domain name that includes a second-level domain (i.e. "website.wix.com") or pay an additional fee to upgrade to your own dedicated domain (i.e. "website.com"). For instance, through Squarespace, you can claim a .com domain name for around $20 per year. Alternatively, you can search for cheaper domain names and connect that domain to your chosen platform.

Please note that not all website-building platforms will have the same policies when it comes to connecting a domain acquired outside of their platform. Therefore, always make sure to check your platform's integration and domain name policies before purchasing a domain elsewhere.

Content Management Systems

A **content management system** (more commonly called a CMS) is a type of software that allows you to create and manage a website in its entirety. Unlike a website building platform, a CMS is fully open-source, meaning you have total control and ownership over your website.

With a CMS, there are several additional considerations for your website, including:

- **Finding a Domain Name:** With a website-building platform, you can receive a free domain name that includes a second-level branded domain that often is the platform's name. Comparatively, with a CMS, you have to obtain your own domain name from a domain marketplace, such as GoDaddy or Namecheap.
- **Choosing a Hosting Provider:** Along with having to find your own domain name, you must also choose a web host. Selecting the right web host is essential, as it can affect how well your website functions and how much hosting support you receive.
- **Keeping Your Site Updated:** When you are in total control of your website, there are many software and application updates you will need to keep up with. If you allow your website to fall behind on new updates, it can become increasingly less functional and glitchy.

One of the most popular examples of a CMS is WordPress.org (not to be confused with WordPress.com, which is the website-building platform version of WordPress). An advantage to using WordPress is that there are many templates and template marketplaces you can use to find a pre-designed website that is available to purchase from a web designer.

For example, Avada (my personal favourite) is a WordPress-based product and template application that allows you to use the WordPress CMS while also benefiting from the more structured elements of a website-building platform. You can do everything from beginner design tasks to more advanced actions like SEO and performance monitoring.

Although creating a website through a CMS is certainly more time-consuming than using a website-building platform, you ultimately gain the benefit of having total control and ownership over your own web content.

Enhancing Your Visitors' Customer Experience

When it comes to customer support on a website, it can be helpful to build a responsive virtual help desk. To do so, you will likely need a hybrid approach that utilizes both chatbots and live chat agents who can assist customers.

Here is a breakdown of the difference between chatbots and live chat agents:

Chatbots

Chatbots are automated software programs — often powered by AI — that have a pre-determined set of responses for specific customer queries.

There are many potential uses for a chatbot, including:

- **Automated Responses:** When you take the time to look through all of the most common questions your support team is asked, you are likely to find a large set of repeated questions. You can input these questions into your chatbot program and create customizable responses that are sent automatically to customers who ask these questions.
- **Qualifying Customers:** Not only can chatbots answer customer questions but they can also ask questions back. As part of an automated response, your chatbot can ask a follow-up question that determines whether or not a customer qualifies as a potential lead for your products and services.
- **Resolving Pain Points:** In most cases, automated chatbots are the first support a customer will encounter on your website. As a result, it is important to make sure your chatbot can resolve common pain points, such as site navigation. Moreover, your chatbot should have the ability to redirect a customer to a live chat agent when a problem is deemed too complex for the bot to handle on its own.

Live Chat Agents

If you have the staff to do so, having a team of people (or person) on standby to chat directly with visitors enables you to provide better real-time support.

Oftentimes, the most successful FinTech websites will have a combination of both chatbot support and live chat agents. Many common questions that customers have when visiting a website — such as navigational questions or inquiries about pricing — can be pretty easily answered by chatbots.

However, for more complex issues that require looking up specific customer data, having a real staff member ready to help is key to keeping that customer's experience positive.

There are many chatbot options available that include both chatbot and live chat capabilities. Moreover, many common chat widgets, like Whatsapp or Facebook Messenger, offer these features and can be integrated into your website.

Boosting Your Website's CRO

If you are creating a website to represent your FinTech company, chances are that one of your main goals is to boost your conversion rates.

What is CRO?

Conversion rate optimization — or CRO for short — is the process through which you optimize your website to increase the number of customer conversions you achieve and the number of leads generated.

In general, there are 3 key principles associated with CRO:

1. **Engage Your Customers:** As you are writing the different sections of your website, keep in mind how each section relates back to your ideal customer. Keep the focus on that ideal customer.
2. **Build Credibility & Incentivization:** For a customer to want to do

business with you, there are two crucial factors to focus on — credibility and incentivization. You have to establish yourself as a trustworthy authority in your industry while also offering a valuable enough incentive for your customers to take action.

3. **Encourage Action:** Along with finding ways to incentivize your customers to take action, you should also encourage action through strategically placed CTAs. I recommend always having a CTA in view on your website.

As for improving your current CRO rates, one of the best steps you can take is to run A/B tests of different landing pages to determine what strategies and language choices work best on your target customers.

There are also prompting tools, like Pathmonk, that use targeted conversation starters on users, that have been shown to increase CRO.

5 Tips for Building a Website that Achieves Your Desired Goals

No matter what types of FinTech products and services you offer, it is critical to always keep your customer at the forefront of your priorities. Your website should act as a catalyst that provides the customer with all the information needed to inspire action.

Here are 5 final tips to remember when building your FinTech website:

1. **Don't Make Your Website Too Distracting:** For the most part, you should stick to the five main sections discussed above when building out your website. Adding too many distracting pop-up windows, unnecessary text, or other elements can turn a customer off and lead them to click away from your website.
2. **Create a Clear Narrative for Your Brand and Customer:** Never forget that you should be guiding your customer through a narrative that positions them as the hero. Keep this narrative clear, with well-defined problems and solutions.

3. **Make it Simple to Contact You:** One of the easiest ways to lose conversions is by making it too complicated to get in touch with you. Ideally, your CTAs should lead to a contact page or you should have a clearly labeled contact page available in your website menu.
4. **Find Ways to Demonstrate Your Credibility:** If you are a new company, you may not have the clientele built up yet to provide positive testimonials for your website. In this case, try to find other key credentials you can include, such as awards, major projects, or years of experience.
5. **Speak to the Needs of the Customer:** At the end of the day, your website should be designed to address the specific needs of your target customer. Focus on personalization.

Above all else, remember that every element on your website should serve a purpose with a primary goal that you are trying to achieve — whether that's converting new customers, building an email list, gauging interest in your products, or anything in between.

Search Engines

"The biggest problem with SEO for any business is that it's generally a slow channel to yield an ROI and is often mis sold and misunderstood. Many young businesses are VC funded – which means the pressure is on to generate new subscribers and MRR – SEO isn't a fast solution for many businesses so many founders/heads of marketing will curtail budget for other channels such as PPC / Social for more immediate results – often allocating insufficient budget – which not only leads to a lack of results – it attracts the wrong kinds of "SEO resource". In more than 95% of cases, budget SEO is bad SEO – because it encourages short cutting for the sake of profit.
If a business can burn through £millions of funding to build the platform and market it on PPC, social media, e-mail and other channels – then it should be able to allocate the right budget to SEO to get real results.
Many businesses that go to market often do not realise the sheer importance of longer term organic traffic growth and opt for the quicker fix – because that's what keeps investors happy. However – it's also the reason why so many businesses have significant organic traffic gaps over time – often heavily relying on blogs and brand traffic – and not attracting traffic from "purchase intent" audiences.
Good SEO isn't about being at the opposite end of the spectrum in terms of budget – cheap SEO = bad, expensive SEO = good – the correlation is good SEO is more expensive when it's done by people with real expertise – not just because they are more expensive to contract/hire, but it's all

the auxiliary costs around it – digital PR for high quality link earning, E-A-T/YMYL aligned content written by people who know the platform, product, market and can construct alluring content that engages – that takes experienced writers who also cost.

Good SEO is the culmination of strategy, practice, patience, and sufficient budgeting."

- Dan Foley Carter, Founder of Assertive, SEO Audits IO & Daniel Foley SEO Consultancy

Search Engine Optimization

I've seen many, many people in many industries get completely screwed by "SEO agencies". It's often small businesses or sole traders, and they always have the same story; the SEO person said everything I was doing was wrong and made me feel like I don't understand anything. They told me I could be ranking within a few days.

On the other hand, I've also seen bigger businesses be very rough on really good SEOs, which has the opposite effect they're hoping it'll have. When an SEO gets you to page 1 in a week, the CEO rejoices, when an SEO person implements a careful strategy that won't get you penalized by search engines and will actually get you leads after 6 months, people feel like the SEO isn't doing anything.

Try to be one of the companies that doesn't get screwed, but also don't miss out on the exceptional rewards having a good SEO person can bring.

There are many great SEO people, but there are also lots of scam artists. So, here's what SEO is, and a bit about how it works, so you can make sure you're one of the people who knows what you're really asking for and will find a great SEO.

Here's a brief explanation of how to do SEO for beginners:

1. Unless you've got access to website developers, use a website that's easily editable, otherwise known as a CMS. For example, WordPress. If you use

WordPress, be sure to add the Yoast plugin. You do not need a custom coded website to be able to rank highly on Google.
2. Find out what people are Googling. Use Answer the Public (free), Google Trends (free), Google Keyword Planner (free but you have to put in your bank details), Ubersuggest (pretty cheap) or SEMRush (more expensive, but lots of other great features).
3. Write a valuable article or webpage that includes the keyword you found in the title, and includes it again in one of the later sub-titles. Don't repeat the keyword anywhere it doesn't make sense to. Your first focus should be the reader.
4. Layout the article in a way that tells search engines what your article is about. For example, put the keyword you used in the alt attribute of your first image (these are found easily in most easily editable websites). Change the meta data (again, can be found easily in your CMS or Yoast) to include the keyword in your title, description of the page, and the URL.
5. Add a few links to other pages on your website that make sense to link to from this page. Go to another page on your website, and use your keyword as the "anchor text" (the text you link from, for example, you might say click *here*, with *here* being the link to a page), and link to the page you are working on. Make sure your anchor text makes sense, includes your main keyword, and that it is useful to the website user to be able to access that page at that moment. Everything comes down to making it easy for the user and providing value.

While there's a lot more to it than that, those are the fundamentals, and a good SEO person or agency will make you feel like part of the process, rather than making you feel like you couldn't possibly understand what they get up to.

Building Links By Building Friendships

Links from other websites to your websites tell search engines you're a trusted site. There's a lot of talk over how to build links. The best way I've found is by building friendships with people in your industry, sending them the occasional article, and asking them if they could link to it from their website. I've also found that this strategy leads to other great results, including making genuine business connections with new people I would never have met otherwise.

Obviously, the real issue here is time. Being a business leader is already very time consuming, let alone having to message countless people on the off chance they'll become your friend and link back to your website from their own.

That's where automation and outsourcing come in. You could use SEMRush to send out mass messages - stick to under 100 a day - or, you can use a virtual assistant to send connection requests from your personal LinkedIn.

The first step is writing a template message. Here's an example you can copy:

Email

Dear Mr. Smith,

It's lovely to meet you. I'm Deborah, Global Head of Marketing at Best Company Inc. I recently read your article on Blue Spotted Birds. I loved it!

I wrote a similar article on Red Striped Birds, I've posted it <here>. I know you probably get these messages all the time, but is there any chance you'd be up for linking to my article from yours? It would really mean the world to me.

Let me know if there's anything I can do for you.

Have a great week.

Thanks,

Deborah

LinkedIn Message

Hi Ms. Smith, my team and I are trying to boost our SEO - I'm sure you know the struggle. I noticed you've got a great blog on Birds, and we'd love to write an article that would provide real world value to your readers. Is this something you'd be open to? Speak soon, Deborah

The caveat to this is that the person you're messaging should know exactly what you're trying to do and why. Be careful with your targeting, the CEO isn't going to appreciate having their precious time taken away for something that doesn't involve them.

However, the Head of Marketing will probably appreciate the hustle, IF and only IF, it feels like you've actually put some thought into the message. Always include their name, always include a nod to their content, and always be brief. No one likes long, drawn out messages. I've made many long-term business connections starting out like this, and the positive effects go well beyond SEO.

Send a message out several times yourself, then tweak your message based on what does and doesn't work. Once you've got a system you're comfortable with, pass the work on to someone else with more time. Keep control over the follow-up conversations BUT if they're not replying, assume they're either not interested, or will get back to you when they're ready. Don't aggressively chase people for links.

Focus on the value of your content

The algorithms are just search engines' way of deciding who gets to the top of the results. The algorithms are actually good for you, as long as you're providing content that is genuinely useful, insightful and easy to read. If you're trying to trick search engines, then the algorithms are bad for you.

Google (and Bing, Yahoo etc.) wants to give its users the answers to their questions. As long as you are answering the question your targeted keyword is asking, trust that Google will realize and boost you up. There have been many occasions where smaller websites have outranked websites with large

SEO teams after an algorithm change, because Google has noticed that the actual content is more valuable on the smaller website than it is on the larger website.

If you experience a drop in ranking, don't worry. That's normal and happens to everyone, including large SEO agencies. Don't try to trick Google. Just focus on improving the content and usability of your website. Make it easy to browse, easy to find the information you need, and easy to read.

Lastly, if you're getting emails telling you you're not ranking, and that for a tidy fee of £200 a month, someone can help get your domain authority up by next week, you're not alone. Every company gets them. Unless you've worked with a dodgy SEO agency in the past, used tactics that break Google's rules, have asked Google to stop ranking you, or have a really weird unusual website, you are probably ranking for something somewhere. Search engines find and categorize most websites. That's their whole thing. The question is what you're ranking for, and how highly. Let Google worry about finding you, you worry about keeping your website users happy.

Key Takeaways

SEO isn't going to cost £200 per month, your agency probably won't get you 2000 links in a week, and you shouldn't be able to jump from a new site to the 1st page on the search engines in a few days.

On the other hand, a good SEO team can add a lot of value to your business, beyond even just marketing, if you let them. For example, they can tell you what's trending right now, and if your competitors have tapped into those trends yet.

If you decide to hire an SEO agency, they should do either all, or some of the following things:

- Find valuable keywords your business should be targeting
- Build relevant links to your site that are genuinely useful for website users
- Find errors in your website, for example, dead links on any of your pages, and correct them

- Optimize each page in line with SEO best practices

When they give you your keywords, have a think about if these are the keywords your customer is going to be interested in, and make sure they show you the search volume per month.

Search Engine Marketing

Search Engine Marketing (SEM) is a powerful tool that belongs in any successful marketing campaign.

For FinTech companies, SEM can be incredibly useful in making initial contact with customers, as well as attracting customers to your business that are ready to make a purchase.

What is Search Engine Marketing & Why Does It Matter?

Search Engine Marketing — commonly abbreviated as SEM — is a marketing strategy that focuses on increasing the amount of web traffic your website or business ads receive on search engine result pages (SERPs).

While SEM can be used for all search engines, it is generally focused on the use of Google's search engine algorithm and website ranking mechanics. SEM primarily deals with paid search advertising, such as the business ads that pop up at the top of a page when you search for specific terms on Google.

What is the Difference Between SEM and SEO?

When developing a digital marketing strategy for your FinTech brand or business, you will likely need to incorporate both paid advertising and methods for drawing in organic web traffic.

The key difference between SEO and SEM is the use of paid advertisements. To gain more traffic and online business using SEO, you have to focus on optimizing your website and creating content that contains many of the relevant search terms customers search for.

Comparatively, SEM allows you to bypass SEO at the beginning, and place your business ads right at the top of a Google search page for a specific keyword or set of keywords.

A Brief Introduction to the Google Display Network

The Google Display Network is a system of more than 2 million different websites, videos, and apps. When you market through the Google Display Network, your ads can appear on any of these millions of different locations, greatly expanding your potential digital reach.

Google Ads is no longer solely focused on displaying your ads on search engine results for specific keywords. With the Google Display Network, you can get your ads on the websites of your choice and on the websites or platforms your users love the most, such as YouTube.

Generally, there are two main types of ads you can use for SEM:

- **Search Ads:** Search ads are the type of advertisements that can appear on a specific search engine result when the right keywords are used by a web user. These ads help you reach the potential customers who are already planning to make a purchase and looking for the right company whose products or services can meet their needs.
- **Display Ads:** Display ads are the type of advertisements that appears across the Google Display Network. While these ads are less likely to appear in front of the most ideal customers who is ready to make a purchase, they are still advantageous in helping you to reach a larger target audience, grow your brand awareness, and gain new leads and prospects.

To use both of these types of ads, you will need to create an account with Google Ads.

How the Google Display Network Works

Once you have set up an account through Google Ads, you can begin using the Google Display Network to determine which audiences your ads will be displayed to.

The Google Display Network uses a strategy known as interest targeting to help you connect with your most relevant customers. On the Google Display Network, there are 3 different types of interest targeting you can select from:

1. **In-Market Audiences:** In-market audiences are web users who are already prepared to make a purchase and are actively searching for a company that has the products or services they seek. When you select in-market audiences, you can reach web users who have searched similar sites or added items similar to yours to their online shopping carts recently.
2. **Affinity Audiences:** Affinity audiences are specific types of audiences that fit within 80 different pre-set categories. This option also allows you to utilize affinity segments that give you a better overview of your target audience's lifestyle, hobbies, spending habits, and more. Affinity audiences can be selected for several different types of Google ad campaigns including display, search, video, and hotel campaigns.
3. **Custom Affinity Audiences:** Custom affinity audiences are a feature within the affinity audiences option that allows you to determine how your ads will reach your target audience. This can include using keywords, URLs, and apps. Custom segments can be set up in display, discover, Gmail, and video campaigns. The custom affinity option gives you greater control over your keywords as well — for example, rather than setting your audience affinity simply as "technology" or "finance," you could instead set it as "FinTech companies in Boston."

In addition to having the ability to select which type of audience you would like to target, the Google Display Network also enables you to set demographic targeting.

Demographic targeting allows you to target people based on their age, gender, parental status, and other demographics. By using this type of targeting in unison with either the in-market or affinity approach, you can further narrow down the audience you are reaching, allowing you to target customers with a much greater level of precision.

Ad Types

While there are many different types of advertisements to choose from, they all generally fall into two categories:

1. **Static Ads:** Static ads only contain the base ad without any additional media or other moving elements in them. These often come in the form of display ads seen as call-to-action buttons or static banners on web pages or videos. Static ads are important to have in your tool belt, as they are more likely to be compatible a wider range of various ad networks.
2. **Dynamic Ads:** Dynamic ads are personalized to a target audience, meaning that they can change depending on who is looking at them. Additionally, dynamic ads also tend to have extra media elements or some level of interactivity that make them more compelling to viewers.

With a static ad, the biggest advantages you have are convenience and ease of use.

Static ads do not take as much time or effort to create compared to dynamic ads. This makes them a great option for use as display ads shown across different websites, social media platforms, and other locations around the web. These types of ads get straight to the point and typically work best on web users who are already ready to make a purchase.

On the other hand, dynamic ads offer you the opportunity to get more creative and make your ads personalized for your ideal customers. These types of ads can help you build more brand loyalty and recognition, as well as attract a wider audience to your business.

Rather than showing every user the same thing as you would with a static ad, dynamic ads allow you to showcase products or services that each individual user is most likely to be interested in.

For example, you can leverage dynamic ads to achieve a retargeting strategy for a customer who has shown interest in your product but didn't sign up. In a dynamic ad, you could promote the same product with a 10% discount if they sign up today.

By segmenting your services into "products", you can get ahead of the competition by utilizing ads that pique genuine interest in users and allow you to run successful ad campaigns that are highly targeted.

Step-by-Step: How to Use Google Ads

To get started with Google Ads, follows these 6 key steps:

Step 1: Create Your Google Ads Account

Signing up for Google Ads is the easy part — you do not have to pay any upfront costs for the software you will be using. Instead, once you start a campaign, you can set your daily budget.

To sign up for Google Ads, visit the Google Ads website and click "Start now".

Step 2: Select Your Campaign Type

After you have your Google Ads account set up and ready, your first step to creating effective SEM ads is to decide which campaign type is right for you.

Google Ads offers 5 types of campaigns:

1. **Search Campaigns:** Search campaigns allow you to create text ads that can appear on search engine results.
2. **Display Campaigns:** Display campaigns allow you to create ads that will reach a wider audience than just those on search engines. Display ads

can appear on websites, apps, social media platforms, videos, and more.
3. **Video Campaigns:** Video campaigns use video-based media as the foundation of the advertisement. These ads are good for boosting brand awareness and showing how your products or services work.
4. **Shopping Campaigns:** Shopping campaigns are designed specifically for selling products, allowing you to feature a product listing in your ad.
5. **App Campaigns:** App campaigns are optimized to appear on mobile and computer apps including on Google Search, Display, Play, and YouTube.

Step 3: Give Your Campaign a Name & Location

Ideally, the name you select for your ad campaign will also contain the primary keyword you are targeting. If it does not, it should still be relevant to the campaign itself.

As for the location, you can cast both a wide and narrow geographic net. If your goal is to target all of the United States, for instance, you can set the U.S. as your location. However, if you are trying to target a specific city within the U.S., you can instead set the location to that exact city.

Step 4: Set a Daily Budget

Google Ads offers two payment options:

1. **Automatic Payments:** With automatic payments, Google will automatically charge your account when an ad is run.
2. **Monthly Invoicing:** With monthly invoicing, Google will provide a line of credit for advertising that will be invoiced to you at the end of the month.

You can also set your daily budget, which determines the amount of money you are willing to spend on advertisements each day. This helps you maintain better control of your ad spend and stay within your overall business budget for marketing.

Personally, I *always* allocate a targeted or specific cost per click, and never allow the cost per click or cost per result to be automated. To do this, choose manual bidding, over automatic bidding, or select a max CPC, and adjust based on results.

Step 5: Choose Your Keywords

Another way you can accrue expenses through Google Ads is with keywords.

According to the official Google Ads keywords page:

"The cost for each keyword will be different depending on the quality of your keyword, your competition in the auction, and other factors. Make sure your keywords and landing page are all closely related to the terms that a customer might be searching for."

Since you will be charged for each keyword you want to use, it is important to make the most of your keywords. Rather than throwing your funds away by purchasing as many keywords as possible, the better strategy is often to invest in a few high-value ones instead.

Step 6: Create & Customize Your Ads

With everything set up and ready to go, you can finally begin creating and customizing your ads.

The Google Ads website offers a free checklist that details everything you need to do in order to set up a Google Ad. Along with taking you through how to choose keywords and set a budget, this checklist also walks you through how to write an ad, set up a landing page, and more.

Once you have your ads created and ready for publishing, you will also want to set up a good tracking tool to monitor your ad performance. Google Analytics is Google's own free product that includes a variety of features for performance monitoring, including:

- Conversions (sales and sign-ups)
- Return on ad spend (SOAS)

- Bounce rate

To use Google Analytics and Google Ads together, you will need to link your accounts. This will allow you to import your data, analytics reports, and more to the platform you are using.

Organic Social

Ever since the invent of MySpace way back in 2003, social media platforms have skyrocketed in popularity. Nowadays, although MySpace is largely a thing of the past, there are more social media platforms than anyone in the early 2000s could have ever imagined — and new platforms are popping up every day!

While social media can be one of the most powerful marketing tools, it is important to understand the nuances of organic social media marketing. Your followers on social media want to feel like they are getting an honest and authentic behind-the-scenes look into your business or brand, rather than constantly being sold on a new product or service.

Start Building Your Social Media Presence in 3 Steps

Think about your favorite social media accounts. What do you like about them? What keeps you coming back again and again for more?

More than likely, the people and brands that come to mind are those that offer authentic experiences and insights into their lives and businesses — and not those who are constantly trying to convince you to buy something every single day.

This is your first important lesson when it comes to social media: leave the selling and advertising for your website and traditional marketing materials.

With your social media platforms, your main goal is to build relationships with your followers. Over time, these relationships will naturally begin to evolve into new customers and business partners.

The basics of building a social media presence are as follows:

- **Pick a Persona, Topic, & Theme:** The most successful social media users and influencers know that it is essential to choose an overall persona, theme, and topic to embody on their platforms. While you shouldn't fake it and act like someone or something you are not, having consistent branding and messaging can go a long way in building a long-term, sustainable audience.
- **Adjust Based on Results:** As you are starting out, your initial approach may not work as perfectly as you want. Though consistency is key, don't be afraid to experiment either — remember, you are just beginning to build your audience and it will take time to do so. Adjusting your online persona and branding based on the results and engagement your receive is essential.
- **Provide Valuable Content:** Content is king on social media, and for that content to produce the results you want, it needs to provide value to your audience. Posts that are all about you, your brand, and your products are not inherently relatable to social media users. Instead, find ways to discuss different topics in FinTech in a way that provides valuable information and insights your followers can keep with them long after initially viewing the post.
- **Focus on Helping Followers Better Their Lives:** Along with providing value through your content, think about how you can influence your followers as well. As a business or brand in FinTech, you hold a level of authority over financial and technology-related topics. Become their guide in improving their understanding of FinTech by identifying their pain points and offering your best advice, guidance, and tips for overcoming them.

Step 1: Choose Your Social Media Platforms Carefully

In the early days of building your social media presence and persona, it can be tempting to create new accounts on every single platform out there.

While it can be a smart idea to create accounts simply for the purpose of claiming your branded username, it is not always the best idea to operate multiple different social media accounts all at once when you are just starting out.

By doing this, you run the risk of spreading yourself thin. In turn, the quality of your content may suffer, diminishing the value you are able to offer and inhibiting you from building a long-lasting audience.

Instead, consider who your target audience is and research which platforms they use the most. Then, create a strategy that focuses primarily on the top one to two platforms where your audience spends most of their time online.

For example, if you are targeting a younger audience like Gen Z, you're going to want to focus on the newer social media sites, like TikTok or Instagram. Gen Z love short-form, engaging content, such as the videos found on TikTok, making this one of the best platforms for attracting their attention.

Alternatively, let's imagine you are trying to target new parents. Social platforms like Pinterest are great for connecting with these audiences, as this is where many new parents go to share updates on their families, join family-oriented groups, and more.

As for a more professional audience — if you are targeting small business owners, for example — opt for more professional social media platforms, like LinkedIn. Here, you can delve into more complex topics with longer-form content that professionals will appreciate and find highly valuable.

Step 2: Develop a Social Media Strategy and Posting Calendar in Advance

The easiest and most effective way to ensure regular social media engagement is to plan ahead as thoroughly as you can.

Here are the 3 key steps for developing your social media strategy:

1. **Create an Annual Strategy:** At the beginning of each year, create a social media strategy in which you review the current state of your social media presence and set new goals for the year to come. This will not only give you clear objectives to work towards but it can also provide you with a better big-picture look at where you are and where you would like to go.
2. **Review & Evolve that Strategy Every 3 Months:** The reality of social media is that it is constantly evolving — and you need to evolve with it. By carrying out reviews of your social media strategy every 3 months and revising your strategy accordingly, you can better keep up with changing trends and evolving audience expectations. After all, nobody wants to be months late to a trend after the hype has already washed away and vanished.
3. **Put Together a Monthly Social Media Calendar:** For most social media platforms, posting at least once per day is a near-necessity. However, trying to come up with these posts the day of is not only time-consuming but can be incredibly difficult, especially if you hit a creative block. Putting together a monthly social media calendar at the beginning of each month will help you in deciding what topics and types of posts you want to create and when the optimal times are to post them.

Planning ahead in this way allows you to allot a few days per month to your social media needs, rather than having to deal with it every single day. As a result, you can save much of your own time or the time of your marketing people while also ensuring you're in the right headspace for creating content.

When it comes to what tools to use for your social media planning, Canva is one of the greatest tools around (seriously, have I mentioned how obsessed

I am with Canva yet?). Not only are traditional graphic design programs expensive but they can also be incredibly complex to use unless you are a designer. By contrast, Canva is easy-to-use, with a drag-and-drop style interface that makes it simple to create infographics, PDFs, and other graphic social posts to share across your accounts.

Plus, Canva allows you to upload your own images and graphics as well, such as your logo.

Other tools for planning your social media strategy include:

- **Hootsuite:** From automatic posting features to social media analytics and market research, Hootsuite has a whole host of capabilities that make social media marketing a breeze. Plus, Hootsuite has Canva integrations that make the two tools a great combo when used together.
- **Google Analytics:** Keeping track of your social media analytics — such as engagement and conversions — is important when reviewing how effective your current social media strategy is. While there are many great analytical tools out there, Google Analytics is a classic, and offers an array of free tools that are incredibly helpful when just beginning your social media journey.
- **Sprout Social:** Sprout Social provides social media software similar to Hootsuite, offering a range of features and products including scheduled posting and engagement monitoring. One great tool you can access through Sprout Social is the social listening product — a tool that allows you to track and keep up with trends, global conversations, industry gaps, and more.

Step 3: Keep Things Simple

As a FinTech brand, you are undoubtedly aware of how complex FinTech topics can get in no time.

The thing is, your target audience may not be comprised of FinTech experts. In turn, one of the best things you can do when building your social media presence is to keep things super simple.

Take complicated ideas and concepts and simplify them for your audience. For example, help your target market learn how to get their first mortgage or how to create and manage a household budget. Alternatively, tackle some of the hottest topics in FinTech today — like cryptocurrencies and NFTs — and help dissolve some of the mystery surrounding these technologies for your audience.

Providing your audience with valuable guidance by turning complicated issues into something simple is the key to building trust and loyalty.

When writing your social media posts and captions, remember to:

- Use short sentences and avoid placing too much information in one social post
- Match the content formatting of the social media platform you're using — for instance, you could write short blog-like posts for LinkedIn and include an engaging picture, but make 15 to 60-second videos for TikTok
- Listen to what your audience has to say and engage with them! Your followers are going to ask you questions in your comments — make sure you are there to answer them and shed light on any persisting confusion they may be experiencing

Additionally, leveraging video content, whitepapers, and blogs across your socials can be an effective way of repurposing material you may already have. As a result, you can save yourself and your brand time and money without taking value away from your audience.

The Growing Importance of Thought Leadership on Social Media

When the pandemic happened, B2B business development within financial markets encountered a problem. In many sectors, sales team members leveraged relationships to make sales. Fancy dinners, lots of wine, and getting to know the client and their family were all great ways to seal a deal.

Suddenly, that all changed — restaurants closed their doors (some were even shuttered forever), businesses began working remotely, and opportunities for in-person networking vanished.

So, what did FinTech professionals do to overcome this challenge?

Enter thought leadership — a strategy in which professionals shared their expertise through the lens of their lived experience and unique perspectives. As the world grew more and more remote, thought leadership rose as a means to continue having meaningful conversations between businesses and their partners and customers.

Social media played a huge role in the rise of thought leadership. Platforms like Twitter and TikTok allowed the thought leaders of the world to share bite-size insights and opinions that then sparked larger conversations, resulting in higher engagement and a growing marketplace for ideas.

Thought leadership removed the emphasis on branding and marketing and placed it instead on the ideas of the individual, even at the business level. By marketing yourself, rather than your company, you create a unique customer experience. With thought leadership, you no longer have to be physically in front of your customers for your customers to feel like they know you.

Financial services have always leveraged relationships, but thought leadership allows you to automate and scale your relationships with business partners and customers in a way that still feels unique and authentic.

The key takeaway here is that leveraging your personal social media to boost business is no longer just the young person's game — professionals from all backgrounds and all walks of life can leverage their lived experiences to become thought leaders on social media, so long as they can maintain a consistent social media persona and strategy.

The 5 Key Social Media Platforms & How to Use Them

Remember that the goal is not to start accounts on every single platform available. Do some research on each, look at the existing content and any gaps that may be present, and then select one to two platforms to focus on.

Instagram

If you're searching for millennials, Instagram is the place to go.

According to Hootsuite, the average user base on Instagram is between the ages of 18 to 44, with this age range making up more than 75% of the total Instagram users. Of these ages, 25 to 34-year-olds use Instagram the most, making up 31.5% of the user base, followed by 18 to 24-year-olds (30.1%) and 35 to 44-year-olds (16.1%).

Instagram is also thought to be Gen Z's favorite social media platform, though TikTok is a close second.

Furthermore, Instagram is nearly evenly split between male and female users. The platform also recently added a preferred pronoun feature that will soon give greater insights into the gender diversity found on the platform.

As for where Instagram users are located, the top 5 nations include India, the U.S., Brazil, Indonesia, and Russia. Indian users are shown to have a particularly high interest in technology-related content on Instagram.

How Often to Post on Instagram

Instagram has three main forms of posts: in-feed posts, Stories, and Reels.

In-feed posts are the standard pictures that appear on your main feed and on a user's profile when you first click on it. Stories are temporary posts that disappear after 24 hours and are featured on a separate feed that users must click on to view. Reels are 15-second videos shown on a side feed featured on a user's profile.

Here is the ideal posting frequency for each of these post types:

- **In-Feed Posts:** It is recommended to post once per day on your main feed. One post per day keeps your engagement up without overwhelming your followers. At minimum, you should aim for at least two to three posts per week if you do not want to post every day.
- **Stories:** Stories are a great way to link out to other content, such as longer-form videos and blog posts. Like in-feed posts, it's a good idea to aim for a story every day, or at least a few times per week. Additionally, you can post more than one story per day without annoying your followers, as viewing Stories is entirely optional. Most brands average between 5 to 10 Stories per day.
- **Reels:** Reels play off the popularity of TikToks, which are short-form videos. Like on TikTok, to find success with Reels, you should post multiple times per week — ideally between 5 to 7. Reels can appear on your followers' main feeds, so still be mindful of how often you are posting and that your Reels do not become a nuisance.

What Types of Content to Post on Instagram

Types of content that tend to perform well on the platform include:

- **Behind-the-Scenes Photos:** As a photo-based platform, Instagram is one of the best social media platforms for offering behind-the-scenes looks into your business or brand's inner workings.
- **Short Video Tutorials:** Many people turn to Instagram for educational tutorials. For FinTech brands, this can include things such as how to create a budget or how to begin investing.
- **Lifestyle Posts:** Lifestyle posts are some of the most popular on the platform and often offer more personal looks into the daily lives of the person or people running an Instagram account. For FinTech brands, this is a good chance to share a lifestyle snapshot and write a short though-leader-esque caption to accompany it.
- **Infographic Slideshows:** Instagram has become one of the biggest platforms for sharing educational infographics, especially when it comes

to social issues and inequalities. FinTechs can take advantage of this form of content to show their deeper values, such as an infographic slideshow on income inequalities and how the gap can be better bridged.

TikTok

Where, oh where, could the Gen Z users be?

Besides favoring Instagram, TikTok is the next biggest app used by this younger generation, with 60% of the user base comprised of people aged 16 to 24. The next biggest group on the platform are older Gen Z and younger millennials, with people aged 25 to 44 making up 26% of the user base.

As for the gender differences on the app, these numbers are close but women ultimately take the cake. Roughly 60% of TikTok's users are female, while around 40% are male.

Interestingly, TikTok has some of the highest levels of engagement and total screen time compared to other social media platforms, making it one of the best platforms for connecting with audiences throughout the day.

How Often to Post on TikTok

When it comes to posting on TikTok, the more the better!

For maximum growth, it is recommended to post between 1 to 3 times daily.

Posting this often can seem like quite the task. Luckily, the average video length on the platform is only about 15 seconds long, despite TikTok allowing videos of up to 3 minutes.

What Type of Content to Post on TikTok?

Though all the content is video, there are many different types of videos you can publish on TikTok.

Here are 4 types of content to post on a professional TikTok page:

- **Trends:** TikTok is full of new trends every day. Participating in these

trends can not only add entertainment value but can help you to gain much greater visibility.
- **Challenges**: Starting a challenge on TikTok is a great way to get users to engage with your content. This includes anything from a dance challenge to a self-improvement challenge!
- **Educational Resources**: Creating short snippets of educational information can be massively successful on TikTok. For example, a credit card company could make a video about 3 tips for saving money or a quick how-to on the ways to improve your credit score.
- **Instructional Videos**: TikTok offers you a great opportunity to visually demonstrate how to use your products or services. By doing so, you can address potential pain points your customers may encounter and provide an immediate solution in your video.

Twitter

Twitter is yet another great platform for connecting with millennials.

Recent demographics show that the largest age group on Twitter is 25 to 34-year-olds, making up 38.5% of the platform's user base. Teenagers are interestingly one of the smallest age groups on the platform, with 13 to 17-year-olds making up just 6.6% of the total user base.

In recent years, there has been an uptick in financial and technology-oriented conversations occurring on Twitter, especially when it comes to cryptocurrencies and other blockchain-related topics.

How Often to Post on Twitter

Like TikTok, Twitter is a great platform for posting short-form content multiple times per day.

In general, you should aim to tweet at least 1 to 2 times per day. Additionally, video content has shown to perform quite well on Twitter, so posting videos a few times per week is recommended.

Typically, you should try to avoid posting more than 5 times per day, as this can be annoying for your followers, and often these posts can end up lost to the ether due to the nature of the Twitter feed. The one caveat here is that, if you are writing a Twitter Thread (more on that below), you can post multiple Tweets consecutively so long as they are part of the same Thread.

What Types of Content to Post on Twitter

Along with standard Tweets, there are a variety of different types of content that Twitter allows for that help boost engagement with your followers.

Some of the best types of content for Twitter include:

- **Threads:** Twitter Threads are a series of connected Tweets that you can add on to at any point after posting. These are commonly used by FinTech brands to discuss financial trends and insights all in one harmonious conversation.
- **Polls:** Twitter allows you to create temporary polls that your followers can vote and participate in. These can be great for asking FinTech-related questions, enabling you to do your own in-app market research and analysis of your followers.
- **Videos:** As mentioned earlier, videos tend to perform well on Twitter. This is great news for anyone who also uses TikTok, as you can simply repurpose your TikTok content on Twitter a few times per week. Don't forget to adjust for the difference in audience.
- **Quote Tweets:** Quote Tweets are a great way to engage with thought leaders in your industry while also adding your own ideas and opinions to the conversation.

Pinterest

Pinterest is an interesting social media platform, as it takes a slightly different form than the others.

Rather than posting a piece of content for users to then comment on, your posts are instead added to your followers' Pin Boards as they see fit.

Additionally, Pinterest is an exceptional platform for getting in touch with older generations, with the largest portion of the user base (38%) being made up of people aged 50 to 64. People aged 30 to 49 make up the next largest group at 34%, followed by ages 18 to 29 at 32%.

From a FinTech perspective, Pinterest is good for sharing educational content, especially anything about personal finance.

How Often to Post on Pinterest

Unlike the other social media platforms, the Pinterest feed curates posts according to each user's individual interests and offers content the algorithm believes they will enjoy.

A user's feed, thus, is not comprised of chronological posts from the people they are following.

As such, you can post many times per day on Pinterest and, in fact, are recommended to do so. The ideal amount of posts to upload to Pinterest per day ranges between 5 to 10.

What Types of Content to Post on Pinterest

Pinterest is a true marketplace of ideas where people go to brainstorm and better themselves.

Content that performs well on the platform includes:

- **How-To Guides & Infographics:** If you are making infographics for Instagram, then consider posting them to Pinterest too — infographics perform well on this platform.
- **Self-Improvement Ideas:** Many people come to Pinterest to create their own Pin Boards for self-improvement on topics of all kinds, from personal finance to fitness.
- **Checklists:** Along the same line of thought as self-improvement ideas, many of Pinterest's users come to the platform looking for pre-made checklists they can follow to improve some aspect of their life. For

example, you could make a checklist on how to prepare to retire early.
- **Educational Content:** Above all, people come to Pinterest for bite-size bits of educational information. From financial advice and literacy to educational FinTech content, this is the place to teach your audience about the world of FinTech.

LinkedIn

LinkedIn is designed specifically for professionals to connect and network with each other.

In terms of demographics, the largest age groups on the platform are 46 to 55-year-olds (37%), 36 to 45-year-olds (34%), and 26 to 35-year-olds (27%). Though the platform does skew towards a male audience, the distribution of male and female users is not too far apart, with around 57% men and 43% women.

Overall, LinkedIn is the place to be for FinTech businesses or brands looking to build B2B connections.

How Often to Post on LinkedIn

On the other social media platforms, most experts recommend posting daily, if not multiple times per day.

By contrast, the ideal posting frequency for LinkedIn is around four to five times per week. Additionally, there are two main ways to post on LinkedIn — as main feed posts or as longer-form articles through LinkedIn's built-in publishing platform.

Keep in mind that LinkedIn is one of the top platforms for thought leadership, so the posts you make on this platform should go a little deeper and more insightful than those you post on other platforms.

What Types of Content to Post on LinkedIn

As mentioned, there are a few different types of content you can post on LinkedIn.

Some of the best to post as a FinTech business or brand include:

- **Short-Form:** Similar to the sorts of posts you might post to Twitter, LinkedIn is a great place for short, vulnerable, witty posts.
- **Newsletters:** To stay more connected with your most loyal audience members, consider starting a newsletter through LinkedIn. This can be anything from a monthly trend report newsletter to a weekly company update newsletter.
- **Video:** Like on Twitter, video content on LinkedIn performs remarkably well. Since the platform is already designed with a professional edge, this is a great opportunity to share videos that provide insights into your company, products, and services. Try to keep things personal and unique, although LinkedIn is a professional platform, personal posts that link back to professional settings do well.
- **Articles/Blogs:** With LinkedIn's on-platform publishing, you can create your own blog and publish your own articles to be shared both on the platform and on other social media sites. This is a great type of content for establishing yourself as a thought leader, but be aware that these tend not to get as much reach as the short-form content.

Paid Social

"90% of our 140+ booked calls a month are inbound from paid ads.

No lead gen forms.

Yes, you read that correctly.

We get most of our meetings from paid ads and yet don't run lead gen forms.

So how is that possible?

We run cold ads to drive targeted traffic to our website (not a lead gen form).

We retarget that traffic with a web of retargeting ads that build trust and credibility with the prospects (not lead gen forms)

– we put case studies, expert advice , client audits, testimonials, expose them to our other online communities, and out our expertise through paid retargeting ads.

The prospects get to know us through our paid ads and multiple visits to our website until they feel comfortable enough to reach out And book a call.

All this talk about demand gen and personal branding is great but not if the assumption is that it's only through organic.

Paid ads are more effective, efficient, and scalable at running the demand gen playbook."

- Justin Rowe, Founder and CMO at Impactable, a LinkedIn Ads Agency

If you only remember one thing about paid social, let it be this: the most important thing about paid social media marketing, is retargeting. Brand awareness is great, but retargeting is where the real magic happens.

The Five Layers of Paid Social

I touched on the marketing funnel in a previous chapter, but it's an essential part of paid social, so I'm going to dive a bit deeper here. Paid social media can be a great way to generate leads and customers, but it's essential to understand the different layers, so that you can create a campaign that achieves your desired results.

What Is The Customer's Journey?

The customer journey is the process that customers go through when interacting with your brand.

Each step of this journey is called a touchpoint. In order to create an effective paid social campaign, you need to know how to approach each touchpoint in the customer journey. Note that this is not a sure science, and it would be best to create a few different versions of your paid social campaigns to see which one performs best.

Awareness

Brand awareness is key, as it helps your customers to become familiarized with your brand name and products. Your ad copy should be clear and concise. Focus on creating a message that is easy to understand and free of industry jargon. Consider using a call-to-action (CTA) that encourages customers to learn more about your brand, such as "Follow Us".

Don't try to sell your products or services in the awareness stage. Instead, focus on building brand awareness, or awareness of a certain issue your customers are facing. Focus on getting potential customers interested in your team or ideas.

Interest

The interest stage of the funnel is where your potential customer is aware of the problem they're facing, and is now aware of a solution to that problem, i.e. your product or service. The interest stage is about building on that relationship with your potential buyer.

It's okay to talk about yourself here, but keep things light, and always focus on adding value. Your potential customer is interested in you, but they're not ready to get married and have babies yet.

Consideration

The consideration stage of the customer journey is when customers start to evaluate their options and consider which products or services they might want to purchase. At this stage, the customer knows they have a problem or a need, and they are looking for a solution. Your ads should focus on how your products or services can solve the customer's problem.

It's important to note that customers in the consideration stage might not be ready to buy yet. They're still comparing their options and considering their needs. For this reason, your paid social ads should focus on highlighting the key benefits of your product or service and showing potential customers how your brand can solve their problems or meet their needs. You might also choose to create marketing materials that compare your solution to that of your competitors.

Conversion

The conversion stage of the customer journey is when customers are ready to take action, such as buying a product or service.

To create effective ads at the conversion stage, you need to focus on using ad copy that encourages customers to take action.

One effective way to do this is to offer a discount or promotion in your ad. This could be a percentage off their purchase, or a free gift with purchase. Another practical approach is to use urgency and scarcity in your ad copy. For example, you might say, "Hurry, the sale ends soon!" or "Only a few left at this price."

At this stage, it's crucial to have a clear call to action that tells customers exactly what you want them to do. Use this as an opportunity to build trust and credibility with your brand by highlighting other customer testimonials or reviews, but don't distract your customer from you want them to do.

Retention

The final stage in the customer journey is loyalty and advocacy. Customers have already converted to your brand at this stage, but you can't forget about them just yet. Instead, focus on building long-term relationships with customers by offering them incentives to stay engaged.

This might include hosting special promotions or events just for your most loyal customers, sending regular email updates that highlight new products or services, or exclusive access to behind-the-scenes content and sneak peeks.

Whatever tactics you choose, the goal is to show customers that you value their business and want to keep them engaged for the long term. Reward them for things like reviews or shout-outs on social media, and use this as an opportunity to collect feedback and ask for their opinions.

How To Move From One Layer To Another?

One of the keys to successfully navigating the five layers of paid social is having a clear strategy in place. To move from one layer to another, you need to identify your target audience, create effective ads and content that resonates with them, and use strategic targeting and retargeting techniques to reach them at each stage of the customer journey.

For the interest stage, you should target customers who interacted positively with your brand in the awareness stage. For example, they might have watched

50% of your first video ad. For the consideration stage, you might target people who are currently googling "your product vs a competitor product".

In the conversion stage, you should target customers already familiar with your brand and interested in your products or services. Maybe they are active on your social media channels, engage with your content, or have asked for more information about your products or services.

Finally, the loyalty/advocacy stage comes after successfully converting customers to your brand; you might get their email addresses off the sales team or CRM system. With a clear strategy for each stage, you can effectively move prospects from one layer to the next until they become lifelong fans of your brand.

Rotating your content is also essential, so people see more than one ad from you, and the worst-performing one is replaced.

Creating Meta Ads

Keeping all of this in mind, let's start with two of the most well-known social media platforms among all age groups — Facebook and Instagram.

Facebook & Instagram Advertising

"Facebook is dead."

Tell that to the almost 2 billion users still on there. I'm not saying you have to market on audience, but getting a strong understanding of who your buyers are, and what platforms they use will help you decide what's best for you.

According to a 2021 report from eMarketer — a digital marketing, media, and commerce market research company — Facebook accounts for almost a quarter of all digital ad spend in the U.S. alone and is forecast to hit an ad revenue value of more than $58 billion by the end of 2022.

On the other hand, many marketing professionals view Instagram as an even bigger opportunity than Facebook. An April 2022 report from eMarketer and Inside Intelligence states that Instagram surpassed Facebook in total ad revenue, accounting for 52.6% of all ad revenue for both platforms combined in 2021 and is expected to account for 60.9% by 2023.

Meta offers an official webpage specifically for amplifying financial services advertising through its platforms. Additionally, Facebook and Instagram offer access to a wide age range of people, allowing FinTech's to reach customers from many different generations.

All this data goes to show that Facebook and Instagram are highly utilized by digital marketers — but how have these platforms been employed for FinTechs specifically?

SoFi — one of the largest digital financial service providers — has seen great success with Facebook and Instagram mobile advertising. According to a 2021 article from Smart Insights, a digital marketing strategy company, Sofi achieved a significant 39% increase in loan applications from mobile ads.

The Smart Insights article states:

"Owing to financial services organizations being rich in customer data, we are seeing an increase in the uptake of custom and lookalike audience modeling on Facebook. Mobile video is popular, including brand discovery via the Explore tab and the use of Facebook Groups, with encouragement from the use of AI."

How to Set Up a Facebook Ad Campaign

Okay, so you're thinking of using Meta, but how do you set up an ad campaign? To begin setting up a Facebook ad campaign, your first step is to get started with Ads Manager.

Ads Manager is an all-in-one tool and advertisement management platform that allows you to create and publish ads, as well as track the performance of your ads, create advertisement budgets, manage an ad schedule, and more.

Through Ads Manager, you can also create personalized ads that are tailored for your specific audience. The Ads Manager tool also provides you with the resources needed to create a tailored marketing plan designed to reach your specific goals as a financial services provider.

Once you are ready to go on Ads Manager, you will need to select the buying type for your ad campaign.

Meta offers two different buying types for ads:

1. **Reach and Frequency Buying:** Reach and frequency buying allows users to purchase and plan ad campaigns in advance, allowing you greater control over your frequency settings. The primary objective of this type of buying is building brand awareness and achieving greater overall reach by boosting traffic and post engagement.
2. **Auction Buying:** Auction buying allows users to experience greater choice and flexibility but at the cost of predictability. While reach buying gives key predictions for reach, spend, and more, auction buying only provides one daily reach prediction. However, auction buying is more effective for reaching a wider variety of marketing goals and can be optimized for a specific objective.

To create an ad campaign with a reach and frequency buying type, follow these 6 steps:

1. Go to your Ads Manager account and select Create.
2. Select Reach and Frequency as your buying type.
3. Select an ad objective — with reach and frequency, only certain objectives are available.
4. Select Continue — this will bring you to the ad creation pane where you will create your ad set.
5. Select Special Ad Categories if your ad campaign relates to credit, employment, housing, social issues, elections, or politics.
6. To finish, you can select either Close to save your ad campaign or Next to create another set.

To create an ad campaign with an auction buying type, follow these 9 steps:

1. Go to Ads Manager and select Create.
2. Select Auction as your buying type.
3. Select an ad objective — all ad objectives are available through auction

buying.
4. Select Continue to bring up the ad creation pane.
5. Enter your campaign name in the campaign name text box — make sure this name is descriptive and compelling.
6. Select Special Ad Categories if your ad campaign relates to credit, employment, housing, social issues, elections, or politics.
7. Create an A/B Test — this is an optional step that allows you to create multiple versions of ads to see which perform better with your target audience.
8. Turn on Campaign Budget Optimization — this is an optional step that allows you to set a daily or lifetime ad budget.
9. Select Show More Options and select Run Ads on a Schedule. Scheduled ads are only available for users who selected a lifetime budget in the previous step.

How to Set Up an Instagram Ad Campaign

As Instagram is owned by Meta — the same parent company behind Facebook — many of the steps for creating ad campaigns on the platform are similar to Facebook's.

To run ads on Instagram, you only need one account on either Facebook or Instagram. If your brand does not have an official Instagram page but does have a Facebook page, you can use this Facebook page to create ads through Ad Manager to run on Instagram.

Alternatively, if you do have an Instagram page, you can connect this account to Ads Manager and create your ad campaign that way.

In addition to setting up either a Facebook or Instagram account through Ads Manager, you will also need to select an advertising objective that allows for ad placements on Instagram.

Once you have determined which objectives best fit your Instagram ad needs, you can begin creating your Instagram ad campaign.

Here are the steps for creating an Instagram ad campaign:

1. Go to Ads Manager and connect either your Facebook or Instagram account
2. Select Create.
3. Choose an ad objective that supports the Instagram placements you want.
4. Select Continue.
5. Fill in your ad set details.
6. Select either Manual Placements or Automatic Placements. Manual placements will allow you to choose exactly where your ads are placed, while automatic placements run your ads across both Facebook and Instagram to give you the greatest value for your ads.
7. Preview your ad and submit it for review.
8. Once approved, your ad will appear on Instagram.

LinkedIn Advertising

LinkedIn is a force to be reckoned with when it comes to B2B marketing, making it a top choice for many FinTechs looking to connect with businesses within the industry.

According to the LinkedIn Marketing Blog, LinkedIn makes up **32% of the market share of all B2B display advertising** and is expected to surpass **$2 billion in U.S. display ad spend by 2023.**

Additionally, LinkedIn is one of the most trusted social media platforms, according to eMarketer's Digital Trust Benchmark Report 2021. The report further states that more than **50% of U.S.-based social media users prefer platforms that protect their privacy and data** and list this privacy factor as "extremely impactful" on their decision to interact with ads.

This is important to note as LinkedIn is generally regarded as one of the top platforms in terms of its ability to protect user data.

With all of this in mind, let's now look at how to create an ad campaign on LinkedIn.

How to Set Up a LinkedIn Ad Campaign

Before you can set up an ad campaign on LinkedIn, you will first need to create a Campaign Manager account.

Campaign Manager is LinkedIn's ad management tool that allows LinkedIn users to create and publish ads. Along with ad creation, Campaign Manager also helps you to set an ad budget, select your ad goals, and manage an ad's timeline.

Additionally, Campaign Manager also offers you a variety of features to get the most out of your advertising campaign, including:

- Dynamic visual reporting for displaying data according to your specific search and filter settings.
- Detailed insights into the viewer actions resulting from your ad campaigns (clicks, likes, shares, comments, and follows).
- Detailed insights into the demographic categories of viewers clicking your ads on LinkedIn.

Once you have set up your Campaign Manager account, you can move on to creating your ad campaign.

Here are the 8 key steps for creating an ad campaign on LinkedIn:

1. Log into your Campaign Manager account. When you create a new account, Campaign Manager will provide you with a tutorial for creating your first ad campaign.
2. Select your objective. LinkedIn offers 3 main objectives to choose from; awareness: focused on building brand awareness, consideration: focused on encouraging customer engagement, conversion: focused on lead generation and lead captures.
3. Build your target audience. LinkedIn allows you to build and save a target audience for your ad campaigns by enabling you to select various professional traits you wish to target (job title, company names, industry type). This is an especially useful feature for B2B Fintechs, as it allows

you to specifically select the financial professionals and customers you wish to get in touch with through your ads.
4. Customize your audience with Matched Audiences. Matched Audiences uses your existing customer data to target the most relevant and valuable customers with your ads.
5. Select an ad format. There are 4 main ad formats to choose between: sponsored content: single images, carousels, and video ads, message ads: ads that appear within the LinkedIn messenger, text ads: right rail and top banner ads, dynamic ads: follower, spotlight, and content ads.
6. Set your initial budget and bid. Your budget helps you to automate or control costs, while your bid amount helps you to reach your target audience.
7. Set up your ad creative — this allows you to generate ad previews in different sizes and environments so you can choose the best options for specific ads.
8. Set up your payment details — you have to enter and save your payment and billing information before an ad campaign can be launched.

TikTok Advertising

Like other social media platforms, TikTok offers an ad program for users looking to promote products and services.

TikTok ads are really low-cost and can be a great way for B2C FinTechs to gain exposure when building an online presence from the ground up.

Not only can TikTok ads help you to grow your audience but they can also provide you with better insights and analytics. They can help you track your customers' behavior and make smarter marketing moves in the future.

While TikTok may not be the most obvious social media platform for advertising your FinTech, it presents a key opportunity you don't want to miss — the chance to connect with younger generations who are emerging as financial customers, or are potentially building a career in financial services.

With TikTok expected to reach roughly 1.5 billion monthly active users by the end of 2022, the time is now for FinTechs to set up effective ad campaigns on the platform.

How to Set Up a TikTok Ad Campaign

Like with Facebook, Instagram, and LinkedIn, the first step to creating an ad campaign on TikTok is to create an account with TikTok's ad management tool and platform.

TikTok Ads Manager enables you to select the primary goals of your ads, set an advertisement budget, and utilize performance-driven solutions. The TikTok Ads Manager offers easy-to-use tools that are beginner-friendly, helping even those who are brand new to the platform create effective campaigns.

Here are 5 steps for creating a TikTok ad campaign:

1. Login to TikTok Ads Manager and click Campaign. From here, click the Create button.
2. Select your ad objective. TikTok offers 3 categories of objectives: awareness: focused on reach, consideration: focused on traffic, app installations, video views, and lead generation, conversion: focused on conversions and catalog sales.
3. Set up your campaign name — your campaign name can have a max of 512 characters.
4. Set your campaign budget. You can choose between 3 budget options: no limit: the No Limit option places no restrictions on ad delivery at the campaign level, though you will need to determine a budget at the ad group level, daily budget: the Daily Budget option allows you to set a daily amount that your ad spend cannot exceed, lifetime Budget: the Lifetime Budget option allows you to set a lifetime amount that your ad spend cannot exceed.
5. Create your ad groups — in your ad group, you can design your ads, determine placement, ad group budget, optimization goal, target audience,

and more.

Best Practices for Effective Social Media Ad Campaigns

Here are 4 best practices to keep in mind when creating your social media ads:

1. **Always Determine Your Target Audience:** As I've have covered, different social media platforms attract different audiences. For a younger audience, use Instagram and TikTok. To reach more mature or professional audiences, use Facebook and LinkedIn. Like anything, rules are there to be broken. So feel free to try marketing to professionals on TikTok, or to kids on Facebook. Knowing who your target audience is, is the key to building the right paid social strategy.
2. **Use High-Quality Visuals:** When you are selecting the media to include in your social media ads, always select high-quality visuals that will leave a positive impression on viewers. Visuals can be a compelling feature that makes a huge difference in whether or not a potential customer clicks on your ad, so make these visuals count.
3. **Keep Mobile in Mind:** As you design your social media ads, keep in mind that many potential customers will view these ads from their mobile devices. This means you should always optimize your ads for mobile displays.
4. **Run Ad Tests:** If you are just getting started with paid social, you may need to do a bit of experimentation to figure out which types of ads and social media platforms work best for your FinTech. Running tests like A/B tests and user device testing can help ensure your ads are optimized and effective.

Events

> *"Events can be a nightmare to put together, and sometimes, everything goes wrong, but at the end of it, the buzz of comradery and elation, not to mention the huge brand recognition and increase in brand affinity you get is worth every second. Just try to mitigate as many risks as you can in advance, and wherever possible, prerecord everything."*

- Ilyas Moumane, Freelance Video Editor and Event Coordinator

For professionals and customers alike, having the opportunity to connect in person or online and learn about FinTech products and services can be a game-changer.

The Value of Experiential Marketing

Experiential marketing is an umbrella term that encapsulates many different marketing techniques, including hosting events. The idea behind experiential marketing is to provide guests with an impactful experience with real-world value.

    This marketing strategy is also sometimes referred to as engagement marketing, as one of the priorities of this strategy is to create an experience that is deeply immersive for guests. The immersive element is what helps to drive business professionals and customers to want to work with your company and brand.

For FinTechs, experiential marketing can be a powerful tool that allows your company to not just connect with your target audience but also to educate your guests on the benefits of your products and services.

Additional benefits of experiential marketing include:

- **Greater Brand Awareness:** Even if a guest at your event does not immediately make a purchase or enter a partnership, they walk away from the even far more aware of your brand. With a well-executed event, you can establish a baseline trust with potential customers and business partners that gives your company better overall recognition and a positive reputation.
- **Increased Customer Loyalty:** Offering a variety of events to your customers and business partners can help you boost your brand loyalty, as you are providing them with something of value in return for their continued patronage. For guests who may be new to your brand, a successful event can help prove to them why they should become loyal to your company.
- **Demonstration Opportunities:** Having your potential business partners and customers gathered together in one place gives you the prime opportunity to present a demonstration of your products or services. This can help give your guests a better idea of what you have to offer and how it can be applied within their daily lives or business.

The Anatomy of a Successful Event

The first key factor to consider is what type of event you want to host. While there are many different types and styles of events, all events can generally be divided into 3 main categories. These event categories include:

- **Small Events:** Small events occur in more intimate settings and are easier to personalize for each individual guest. For a small event, your guests

will typically include high-level professionals of businesses you want to work with, long-time customers, and notable prospective customers.
- **Large Events:** Large events occur on a much bigger scale, allowing for more extravagant activities but less customizable experiences for individuals. Your guest list for a large event will consist of existing and prospective customers, business partners, and relevant industry professionals. These types of events create great platforms for networking, presenting, and educating.
- **Online Events:** Online events are essential for your event marketing repertoire, as they not only accommodate businesses that work remotely but they also help you to connect with potential partners and customers all around the globe. With an online event, you are not restricted to a specific date, time, or location, giving you more flexibility in your event planning.

Here are 5 important elements that make up the anatomy of a successful event:

1. **Structure:** The core structure of your event is one of the most crucial elements to focus on figuring out first, as this will define how you plan your event activities, speakers, presentations, and everything in between. Properly structuring an event requires you to develop a detailed plan that includes everything from venue layout to activity scheduling.
2. **Concept:** Any event you host should have a core concept that it is built around. For instance, if you run a FinTech company that focuses on payment processing, you may want to coordinate an event around how small businesses utilize your payment technology. The concept behind this event could be supporting small businesses, allowing you to involve a wider range of participants and guests.
3. **Content:** No event is complete without well-planned content that is on theme with your event concept and fits well into your event structure. A good event will offer a variety of different types of content including short videos or films, in-person presentations and speakers, and product demonstrations.

4. **Sponsorship:** Generally, throwing an event will require you to have a budget. As such, instead of solely relying on your own company's funds, you can use this as an opportunity to network with other relevant FinTech companies and find businesses willing to sponsor your event. In return, you can feature the sponsors via branded merchandise or as keynote speakers.
5. **Audience Targeting:** You never want to throw a generic event — whether your event is small or large, it should always be tailored and targeted toward a specific audience. Even if your event involves a variety of different guests including both clients and business partners, ensuring the event content, concept, and activities are highly relevant to your guests is key.

How to Plan an Event Budget

One of the best tools for creating and tracking a budget is Microsoft Excel, as you can clearly map out what you need to allocate funds towards and update the spreadsheet on how much you actually spend. Having a well-organized Excel spreadsheet will help you to track and record your expenses, allowing you to better analyze the success of your event afterward as well.

Important event costs to consider include:

- **Venue:** If you have an event space at your business, then venue costs will be minimal. However, for most in-person events, you will need to rent out or reserve a venue that has the space and resources for the event you are planning.
- **Food & Drink:** We have all heard the joke "Will there be food?" when telling someone about a work-related event. Include either purchasing pre-made food and drinks or hiring a catering service in your budget.
- **Invitations:** No event is complete without its guests — but you won't have guests without a proper invitation. These days, you can forego the

costs of printing physical invitations in favor of sending out digital ones instead. It is still important to consider these invitations in your budget, however, in case you choose to use an invitation design tool that costs money, or an electronic system for processing people's entry.
- **Marketing**: While the event itself may be part of a larger marketing strategy, you also need the right amount of marketing to attract people to your event. Unless your event is invitation-only, you will need to utilize a variety of marketing methods to convince your target audience to attend — from email marketing to social media promotion.
- **Presentation Equipment:** If your event involves speakers and presentations, it is important to have the right equipment handy to ensure each presentation has great sound quality. Additionally, your presenters and speakers may want to show visuals as part of their presentation, so you may need projectors and other visual equipment.
- **Staffing:** For smaller events, you may only need one or two staff members to help out with event organization and coordination. For larger events, having event staff available is crucial for ensuring the event runs smoothly, directing guests to the right locations, and answering guest questions.

Once you have listed out all of the costs involved in your event, it's time to begin planning the actual budget. To do this, follow these 5 steps:

1. **Determine a Minimum & Maximum:** Setting one, singular number for an event budget might be a bit tricky, as many variables can change at a moment's notice and upset your entire event budget. Instead, create a minimum and maximum budget you are willing to spend and plan for both of these budgets. Get online, and get some quotes from suppliers to help improve your predicted budget.
2. **Analyze Past Budgets:** If you have hosted events in the past, analyze your past event budgets to discover where you need to spend more or less money. For companies who have never hosted an event, research events of similar size and nature to get a more precise outlook on how much you should plan on spending for each event cost.

3. **Set Clear Monetary Goals:** Always set clear monetary goals when creating your budget. To know how successful your event is, you need well-defined budgetary boundaries, including how much you hope to spend vs. how many sales you hope to land during the event. Knowing how much money you hope to gain can help you determine how much you are willing to spend.
4. **Consider Unexpected Costs:** Even with a detailed list of potential costs, unexpected expenses will almost always occur when planning an event. Setting aside a portion of your budget for unexpected costs is the key to keeping your head above water during an event when different variables may work against you. I like to allocate 15%.
5. **Create a Contingency Plan:** Having a contingency plan in place that accounts for worst-case scenarios is essential. For the safety of your guests — and to legally protect your business — it is important to consider how you will deal with negative occurrences at your events, such as injuries or food poisoning.

As you search for suppliers, it is important to take your time to compare them against each other. This means you will need to plan well ahead of time so that you have ample time to request pricing quotes and shop around. I like to give myself 3 months to plan any event.

With your budget and suppliers in place, you can now begin planning the actual event. After you have chosen the type of event you want to host — small, large, or online — you can begin the coordination process.

Coordinating a Small Event

Small events offer the opportunity to create a more intimate and exclusive environment for your guests. These are the types of events that you can make invitation-only, making the whole experience feel more special and unique.

With a small event, you will need to place greater emphasis on the individual experience while planning. Small events can be some of the most memorable experiences for both you and your guests, giving you the chance to network with your most important customers and business partners.

To do this, follow these 7 steps:

1. **Embrace Micromanagement:** I know, this is usually something we avoid. But unless you're hiring an event agency, it's essential that you stay on top of everything. For a small event, you have more opportunities to check in with your event staff — whether it's your caterers or your tech managers.
2. **Plan Individual Experiences:** Small events enable you to consider the experience of the individual over the entire group. Having the right content and speakers can help you to create an experience that is tailored for the individuals who are in attendance, rather than planning more general content that can suit the masses.
3. **Offer Conversation Starters:** This is where the real event comes together. In a small event setting, conversations between attendees can drive the success of the event. Try to lead the conversation, and help your guests feel more comfortable getting to know one another and network. If you can guide the topic onto one of the pain points your business helps solve, all the better.
4. **Create an Intimate Ambiance:** Unlike a large event, a small event allows you to pay more attention to the overall ambiance. From lighting to seating arrangements, everything at your event contributes to the ambiance. At a small event, you want this ambiance to be very welcoming, encouraging guests to roam around the event space and communicate with you and other guests.
5. **Make It Invitation-Only:** Making a small event invitation-only will help you to ensure you can accommodate all of your guests properly. Plus, it gives the event a greater sense of exclusivity that can make your guests feel special and appreciated. I like to stick to 10-14 senior individuals, with a mixture of clients and prospects. To get this number, I usually invite 20-30 people, and assume about half will accept.
6. **Include Interactive Demonstrations:** Small events offer some of the

best opportunities for showcasing interactive demonstrations where you can show off a product or service, as well as let your guests interact with it themselves. This is especially useful if you have a tech-based product that you hope to showcase, as you can show guests exactly how it works and then let them try it out on their own and directly answer their questions as they arise.
7. **Staff Accordingly:** Staffing for an event ultimately depends on what types of activities and services the event offers. At minimum, a small event should have staff members responsible for overseeing food and drinks, for operating presentations and other technology, and for admitting guests to the event at the front entrance.

Example of a Small FinTech Event

To help you better picture what a small FinTech event may look like, let's examine the following example of a wine tasting for a B2B FinTech.

A wine tasting is a great option for a small event, as you can reserve a winery venue space that is already designed to provide a beautiful and welcoming ambiance. Plus, who doesn't love free drinks?

At a wine tasting, your main focus should be on creating an open-ended environment that encourages conversation and networking. While your guests learn about and taste different wines, you can easily ignite conversations between them with a variety of ice breakers and conversation starters.

Additionally, having demonstrations set up around the space can help you show off the B2B technology you have to offer. Take this a step further by using your technology to help support the winery staff during the event, giving you a built-in demonstration to reference with a real-life example of how it can be applied at a business.

For this type of wine tasting event, it is important to have a sommelier present for at least the first 30 minutes to an hour. While you want to have ample opportunity to discuss your own products and services, having a winery expert like a sommelier will help you to create a wonderful non-work-related experience for your guests.

Coordinating a Large Event

Compared to small events, there is much more planning involved when coordinating a large event. Not only do you need to plan accordingly to accommodate a much larger audience but you must also find ways to keep the event interesting and engaging even when you cannot speak with each individual guest.

Moreover, there are more chances for failure at a large event, so having the right contingency plans in place will help you ensure that the event is successful and that small flaws are contained and dealt with quickly.

Here are 7 steps for coordinating a large event:

1. **Make It Impactful:** At a small event, it is easy to leave an impact on your guests as you can speak to them directly. For larger events, you need to find ways to achieve a similar level of impact through your event activities, presentations, and ambiance. One good way to do this is by allowing guests to customize their own schedules to some degree, enabling them to select which activities or demonstrations they are most interested in attending during the event.
2. **Create a Hashtag:** To help build a sense of community at your event, create a special hashtag that is specifically for your guests to use on social media. This will not only help your guests to communicate with each other but can also result in some great social media marketing.
3. **Incentivize Participation:** Larger events can feel more intimidating to participate in for guests. One of the best ways to create a feeling of belonging is by incentivizing the use of your hashtag — you can offer prizes to the best social media posts or most active hashtag users, encouraging your guests to interact with each other both in person and on social platforms in an effort to win a prize.
4. **Plan Seating Arrangements & Gathering Spaces:** Unlike a small event where you may have just one or two communal spaces, a large event will likely have multiple different areas for guests to wander around. To make the most out of your venue space, make sure to coordinate more

organized seating arrangements for presentations or demonstrations, as well as more open areas for guests to gather and converse with each other.

5. **Find the Right Caterer:** When it comes to food at a large event, it's better to have too much than too little — especially if the event will take place for more than just a couple of hours. Consider speaking with local foodbanks to discuss donating any food that isn't served, do this in advance, as foodbanks often need to be warned of large intakes.
6. **Place Support Staff Around the Venue:** Depending on the size of your event venue, it may be easy for guests to become turned around looking for a specific activity — or even just looking for the bathroom. Strategically placing support staff around the venue will help you to ensure each guest is directed to the right location, as well as allow you to direct guests to specific activities, presentations, or demonstrations that you feel are most important.
7. **Include More Business Associates:** Large events require you to be running around constantly, which can take away from how much time you have to network with your guests. As such, having other business associates from your own company present can help you to ensure there is always someone around to speak with guests and answer their questions.

Example of a Large FinTech Event

One of the best examples of a large FinTech event is a product launch event.

At a product launch, the main focus of the event will be your company's new product or service. Your key activities will include product demonstrations, keynote speeches from yourself and your team, and question and answer sessions for your guests.

Additionally, an event like a product launch gives a good opportunity to either record the event to post online later or livestream the event to online audiences. This helps you reach an even wider audience than those who are able to attend in person, allowing them to feel like they are still a part of the fun and appreciated by your brand.

Creating an Online Event

Unlike in-person events, an online event will not require you to have catering, support staff, or an event venue. Instead, you will need an online platform capable of supporting many different users from different areas of the world all at once.

This ability to make your event more global is also one of the greatest advantages of hosting an online event. After all, you can reach a much wider audience without asking them to travel to your location.

Planning an online event can be much more technical, as you want to make sure all of the technology involved runs smoothly. However, you still need to be conscious of the experience you are creating and how you can make this experience engaging for your guests.

Here are 3 key steps for planning an online event:

1. **Choose Your Event Tech:** For an online event, technology is at the heart of your event's success. Along with standard tools and video-recording programs, like Zoom, you also need a variety of tech that will help you to create a personalized experience for your guests. I use BigMarker integrated with a CRM to run my events. You can also use tech to create a more unique experience, for example, you can create a mobile app specifically for your event that includes information on speakers, presentations, schedules, registration, and enables attendees to speak to one another in forums. Wix App Builder could help with this.
2. **Decide Between Live or PreRecorded:** When hosting an online event, you have the opportunity to offer content that is either prerecorded or live. Both have advantages and your online event will likely include a mix of the two. The key deciding factor is how much audience participation matters for a specific activity or piece of content — if participation is highly important, such as during a Q & A, then you will want to opt for live content. However, prerecording gives you greater control over your content and helps you to avoid problems that can occur with live streaming. I've found a lot of online events are actually prerecorded,

and would definitely suggest prerecorded for most online events, for example, webinars and speeches.
3. **Find Ways to Enable Audience Participation:** Unlike in-person events, your audience members cannot just walk up and speak with you or other guests. To meet this dilemma, you will need to use tools that enable chat features and can help you build customizable virtual chat rooms.

Example of an Online FinTech Event

One of the best types of online FinTech events is a virtual conference, as this will give you ample opportunity to incorporate both live and prerecorded content.

For major presentations and demonstrations, you can easily prerecord this content and showcase it during your online event. To make this feel more personal for your viewers, you can follow up your prerecorded event with live Q & A sessions in which audience members can directly participate through your virtual chat features.

Plus, online conferences can give you the same opportunity as large events to create a hashtag and encourage guest participation on social media.

Influencer Marketing

"If you want to be successful on LinkedIn, you need to remember that people are more interested in WHO you are, HOW you do what you do, and WHY you do it, before they become interested in WHAT you do. Doing this builds trust and an emotional connection with your business, which is crucial for attracting leads on LinkedIn."

- Lea Turner, Founder of Lea Does LinkedIn, a LinkedIn Training Workshop

In the early days of influencers, the businesses most likely to engage in influencer marketing were fashion, health, and beauty brands. These brands found success with influencer marketing as the products and services they offered were in line with what popular influencers were creating content around.

Now that social media has grown, more industries are discovering the potential of influencer marketing — including the FinTech industry.

Top FinTech Influencers

Whether you are looking for an influencer to work with or searching for inspiration to begin your own journey to becoming an influencer, looking at some of the leaders in the space is a good place to start.

Overall, LinkedIn offers one of the best social media environments for

FinTech influencers to thrive, with some of the top influencers in the space acting primarily from this platform. Twitter is often a strong companion for LinkedIn, as it helps reach a wider audience.

Here are 3 examples of notable FinTech influencers on Twitter and LinkedIn:

- **Spiros Margaris:** Spiros Margaris (@SpirosMargaris on Twitter, in/spirosmargaris on LinkedIn) is a venture capitalist and the founder of Margaris Ventures. With 120K+ followers on Twitter and 13K+ on LinkedIn, Spiros uses his platform to share some of the latest news, opinions, and innovations coming out of the FinTech industry.
- **Theodora Lau:** Theodora Lau (@psb_dc on Twitter, in/theodoralau on LinkedIn) is an author and the founder of Unconventional Ventures. Theodora also works as an advisor and public speaker, giving her the right mix of skills and expertise to inspire confidence within her audience. On LinkedIn, Theodora publishes a newsletter titled The FinTech Prose that has more than 30,000 subscribers. Her work has even been acknowledged and published by the MIT Technology Review.
- **Brett King:** Brett King (@BrettKing on Twitter, in/brettking on LinkedIn) is well-known in the FinTech industry and works as an author, speaker, and podcast host — among other things. Brett is a thought leader in the FinTech space, looking at the larger implications of FinTech and how it can shape society.

As for Instagram and TikTok influencers, key distinctions set them apart from Twitter and LinkedIn.

Many influencers on Instagram and TikTok will appeal to their audience's personal struggles with finances and financial technology rather than writing in-depth opinion pieces.

As such, many influencers do not take solely a FinTech approach but rather create a variety of content on all sorts of relevant topics, from financial advice to crypto explanations.

Here are 2 examples of Instagram and TikTok influencers in the FinTech space:

- **Humphrey Yang:** Humphrey Yang (@humphreytalks on TikTok and Instagram) is a massive creator and influencer in the financial side of social media. With 500K+ followers on Instagram and more than 3.3 million on TikTok, Humphrey has a massive audience with which he shares financial and investment advice. This includes many FinTech topics, including keeping your money safe on money transfer apps like Venmo and explanations of cryptocurrency and NFTs.
- **Parii Bafna:** Parii Bafna (@pariibafna on TikTok, @thepariibafna on Instagram) is a financial advice influencer who researches and provides educational information to their audience, including tips for building credit and how to get into mobile banking. Parii has more than 300K followers on TikTok.

How to Work with Influencers

Here are 5 tips for working with influencers as a FinTech company:

1. Research Influencers Thoroughly

There are influencers of all kinds on every platform. When you are selecting influencers to reach out to, it is critical to thoroughly research them beforehand to make sure their content matches the overall style, tone, and branding of your company.

Making sure the influencers you want to work with are targeting your ideal audience is key.

Be cautious of influencers who have fake followings.

Many people have seen the appeal of social media jobs, leading some to try to fast-track their way to the top by paying for bot followers. Although every account on almost all social media platforms has a small number of bot followers, influencers paying for these bots will have considerably more.

One of the best ways to determine if an account has mainly bot followers is to look at their follower count vs. their engagement. For instance, if an account has 200,000 followers but only 10 likes per post, there's a good chance they have a hefty serving of bots in that follower count.

A smaller creator who only has a few thousand followers, but loads of consistent engagement would likely make for a much better investment.

2. Reach Out to Influencers in Your Field & Industry

After find the right influencers, reach out to them.

Even if these influencers are not currently open to new brand partnerships, they may be able to offer recommendations. Plus, reaching out to a variety of influencers can help build brand name recognition amongst some of the most popular social media users in the FinTech space.

Along with working with influencers who are big in the FinTech niche, consider reaching out to relevant industry professionals with large, relevant, or targeted followings as well.

3. Approach Influencers Respectfully

Before you approach an influencer about a potential partnership, it is crucial to plan out what to say. Brands have been called out publicly for approaching influencers rudely or expecting free work.

To put it simply: Speaking to influencers without the proper level of respect you would pay to any other professional is the best way to fail at an influencer marketing campaign.

This is especially true when dealing with influencers in the FinTech space. Many FinTech influencers are professionals in the field who have years of experience and expertise to back up and validate their content. If you approach such an influencer disrespectfully, it could be disastrous for your reputation.

4. Clearly Outline Your Expectations

Every influencer is different —so your approach to working with each individual influencer needs to be thorough and clear-cut.

Starting a new influencer partnership is similar to hiring a new freelance or contract worker. They work according to the standards and expectations you set as the employer/client, and they may only put in the amount of effort that you specifically ask for.

As a result, it is important to provide clear guidelines for exactly what you want an influencer to say in promotional content.

It is also a very wise idea to write up an official contract with these expectations concisely listed.

5. Ask About Promotional or Sponsorship Costs

Once you have started a conversation with a FinTech influencer and asked about what types of promotional services or partnerships they offer, your next key step is to ask for a price quote.

Depending on how the influencer handles brand deals, you may be discussing this with just the influencer or with the influencer and their manager. In many cases, brand deals become negotiations of sorts in which you state your ideal budget and the influencer and their team offer their ideal price.

Remember — you are dealing with professionals.

Social media promotions, marketing partnerships, and sponsorships make up a large portion of most influencers' income, so you are unlikely to receive such services for free — nor is it considered good form to ask an influencer to work for you for free.

How to Build Your Own Audience on LinkedIn

Aside from working with established FinTech influencers, you can also strive to become a FinTech influencer yourself. Becoming an influencer is no small task and requires a lot of time, commitment, and patience, but it can reap tremendous rewards for those who stick to it.

Here are 5 tips for becoming a LinkedIn FinTech influencer:

1. Write a Catchy LinkedIn Headline

Directly under your name on your LinkedIn profile is a section where you can write a profile headline.

This headline is important, as it helps you create a positive first impression on anyone visiting your LinkedIn page. A headline also gives you the chance to concisely explain who you are, what you have to offer, and why it is beneficial to work with or follow you.

To write your headline, consider what your value proposition is — aka, what is the most valuable feature about you as a FinTech professional and influencer that you want followers to notice.

A headline should be short and sweet, ideally between 100 to 200 characters in total.

To take your headline to the next level, you can even create a banner image that either states your headline or your business name in a legible script. This banner could also be a good place to list your products or services.

Even if you are no pro at graphic design, you have several online tool options that can help you create an attention-grabbing banner. One of the best is Canva (I've probably mentioned Canva a million times so far, and will continue to do so, because Canva is the best), a drag-and-drop design tool that is intuitive to use and can create a wide variety of content beyond just banners.

Include an email address, website, or call to DM in your banner.

2. Test & Retest Your Approach

As you get more comfortable, testing out different styles of posts and content can help you determine what your audience is most interested in.

For example, let's say you run a FinTech company and are promoting the upcoming release of a new mobile app for business budgeting. To test out different types of content, you could write a LinkedIn post in the style of a press release, create an infographic, and try out a short explanation video.

By posting multiple forms of content on several different platforms, you can compare the performance of your various accounts in real-time. This also gives you the chance to test out different hashtags to figure out where you are gaining the most traffic from.

3. Change Your Professional Title to Something Searchable

On LinkedIn, there is a special category just for you to list your professional title.

Choose a professional title that not only accurately portrays what you do but also contains clear and search-friendly language. Choose a title that includes the words you want to sell – for example, I've put "FinTech writer" in mine, so that anyone searching for a fintech writer will come across my page.

4. Keep Up with Posting for at Least a Year

To put it bluntly, building up a social media following takes time.

Some influencers get lucky with a viral piece of content that drives thousands of new followers to their page — but these influencers often have experience that enables them to create content that builds up a following so quickly, they also have to put in the effort and elbow grease to keep those followers engaged long-term.

Moral of the story: To become an influencer, you have to put in the work and earn your audience.

Whether you already have a decent following or are starting from scratch, to see consistently positive results coming from your influencing efforts, you should aim to keep up with a regular posting schedule for a minimum of one year.

This doesn't mean you can cut the consistency after this first year, it only means that it can take upwards of one year to begin seeing the results you want.

Ideally, your goal should be to post a unique piece of content to your social channels at least once per workday to keep your audience engaged and interested. After all, follower retention matters arguably more than follower attraction.

5. Follow & Interact with Other Influencers in Your Industry

If you want to establish your presence as an influencer in the FinTech industry, then you have to pay your dues by following and supporting other creators in the same space as you.

Follow FinTech pros on your chosen social media platform, including those who talk about similar topics and products as you do. Prioritize following accounts with a large following but do not underestimate the power of following smaller accounts — this can often lead to a network of peers who help uplift and support each other's content.

Most importantly, engage with the content of the people you follow. Leaving thoughtful comments not only pays respect to your peers but also gives you greater exposure.

Press

When it comes to boosting your brand awareness as a FinTech company, there is no tool more powerful than a good dose of positive media attention.

Media and public relations (PR) professionals are always looking for the next big story, especially when it comes to industries that can affect the daily lives of their audience. As FinTech deals with both the growing importance of technology and the need for effective financial services, FinTech companies often find themselves in the PR spotlight — for better or for worse.

The key to receiving positive media attention lies in having an intentional approach to PR. Rather than allowing the media to concoct a story about your company after a major event has occurred, it is crucial to stay a step ahead and control the narrative whenever possible.

The Importance of Positive Media Attention

For companies in all industries, building brand awareness is essential to attracting more customers and business partners.

Positive media attention is one of the best ways to gain this brand awareness, as it not only helps give your company a great reputation but also exposes new audiences to your company as well. However, on the other hand, negative media attention can produce the opposite result, giving your company a bad reputation and turning customers away from your products and services.

To help better illustrate the effects of positive vs. negative media attention,

I've detailed a few examples of both below:

FinTech Companies Excelling at Good PR

Some of the key factors that go into good PR include:

- **Simplicity:** A long and complicated story about exactly how a product or service works is not going to stick with an audience, but an inspiring tale about how a FinTech company helped to support a small business certainly will.
- **Customer-Centricity:** The ability to frame your company's media coverage to highlight how well you prioritize customers is crucial.
- **Education:** Customers are automatically drawn to FinTech companies that demonstrate a commitment to providing educational resources for customers to become more financially and technologically literate. As you plan your media and PR approach, keep in mind how you can educate the public for the better.

One of the best examples of a FinTech company that encompasses all of these key factors for good PR is Stripe.

The business leaders at Stripe have taken a very proactive approach to media and press, often responding to both positive and negative PR very quickly and effectively. Stripe focuses heavily on providing customer-centric marketing and educational resources by staying in touch with customers online, be it through social media or Stripe's own virtual conferences known as Stripe Sessions.

This connectivity to their customers makes it easier for the company to maintain brand loyalty, even in the event of bad press.

For example, in a 2022 article from CNBC addressing the accusation that Stripe participates in "unfair competition" with its rival companies, quotes from Stripe's president John Collison during a Money 20/20 conference in Amsterdam focus heavily on the needs of customers rather than the backlash from Stripe's competitors. One such statement from Collison includes:

"Sometimes there will be someone else in the market with a product like Plaid and then we will enter a space with a similar product but with pure differentiation for customers."

Understanding the importance of speaking to the needs and hearts of your customers is a core principle to turning even negative PR into something that works in favor of your company.

FinTech Companies & Bad PR: A Cautionary Tale

While good PR can be an excellent tool when employed correctly, bad PR can spell disaster for even the biggest FinTech companies.

Bad PR can occur for a number of reasons, including:

- **Poor Customer Service:** For many FinTechs, one element of business that can sometimes be overlooked is customer service. While your services may offer key advantages like accessibility and convenience, for many customers the innovation of FinTech may still be relatively new to them. A strong approach to customer service can help avoid bad PR.
- **Overly Complex Technology:** FinTech can quickly become overly complicated if a company is not careful about optimizing its user experience and making its products and services intuitive. All the good marketing in the world cannot save you from a product being too complicated, leading to negative reviews and potentially, bad press.
- **Unethical Practices:** One of the biggest ways a FinTech can get itself in trouble with the press is by enabling unethical practices to take place. As you will see in the example below, a perceived lack of ethics can lead to major downfalls that not only result in bad press but also lead businesses to legal trouble and lawsuits.

One example of a FinTech company that received bad PR is an investment mobile app many use to trade in stocks, ETFs and cryptos.

Since its founding, the investment app marketed itself as one of the leaders in the movement to make investment and stock trading more accessible to all people. Before facing a major scandal in 2021, it promoted its services as a way to democratize finance.

That all changed 2021 when the infamous GameStop Short occured, causing the GameStop stock to rapidly ascend more than 600% in less than a week's time. Among the many consequences of this event included more than $19 billion lost in hedge fund assets, as well as a mixed bag of results for individual investors who chose to partake in this once-in-a-lifetime scenario.

Where this app fits into this equation is that the stock exchange chose to prevent trading of GameStop, stopping many of its users from buying more than one share of the stock. This caused an uproar amongst investors of all kinds, as up to this point the company had touted its ability to enable fair and free trading for everyone.

When the app released its formal blog article addressing the situation, the company cited significant market volatility as the main reason for its decision to restrict trading. Yet, despite their best efforts to state that the actions the company had taken were in the best interests of its users, many felt the damage was done.

According to the press around the time, a platform that had once been hailed as a platform for the people was now the subject of great criticism and backlash from people on all ends of the investment spectrum. Some investors even went so far as to sue them, accusing the company of colluding with other financial companies to stop the loss of money occurring in major hedge funds.

While the company ultimately won the lawsuit, several media sites claimed they lost more than 1 million users from 2021 to 2022 and experienced a 73% decrease in revenue from equities trading.

The Lesson to Learn

One takeaway someone could take from the Investment Apps situation is to not market services that you do not have the resources to provide for users.

While no one could have predicted the outrageous nature of the GameStop short, many felt the investment app ultimately failed its users by going against the very financial accessibility it had marketed for so long. This is potentially an important lesson for FinTech companies not to make promises that you are unsure you can keep up with long-term.

Even after winning the lawsuit brought against it, many felt the company still suffered from major user and revenue losses, proving that even when you are deemed legally in the right, your company can still lose its hard-earned audience once that audience has felt their trust has been broken.

The Role of Guerilla Marketing in FinTech

Guerilla marketing is an unconventional form of marketing that aims to generate buzz and PR about a specific company by using low-cost, memorable tactics.

This form of marketing is very reliant on the media and press, as heavy coverage of the tactic is a major component of what makes this marketing strategy successful. In many cases, guerilla marketing will make use of social media to create a viral moment that catches the attention of the press.

A great example of a successful guerilla marketing tactic is WePay's direct call-out and confrontation of another payments company that went viral back in 2010.

As part of this marketing ploy, WePay constructed a 600-lb. block on ice that contained several hundreds of dollars, with the all-caps message saying that their competitor "FREEZES YOUR ACCOUNTS. UNFREEZE YOUR MONEY" at the top of the ice block.

According to a report from HubSpot, WePay officials reported that the stunt resulted in a 225% increase in sign-ups, as well as a 300% in weekly online traffic and roughly 3 times the number of conversions on the following day.

To start your own guerilla marketing campaign as a FinTech company, make sure to follow these 3 essential steps:

1. **Develop an Original Idea:** The key element to a successful guerilla marketing campaign is an original idea not commonly seen in other

marketing campaigns. Your idea should be thought-provoking.
2. **Know Who Your Target Audience Is:** Given that guerilla marketing is quite targeted in its messaging, you need a clear idea of the exact audience you are trying to reach. This will help you conduct better research and develop a campaign that speaks to this audience's biggest concerns, frustrations, or desires in the FinTech industry.
3. **Be Provocative, Not Offensive:** Guerilla marketing toes the line between being provocative and offensive, especially when it comes to more viral call-out moments like the one seen with WePay. Your goal should be to provoke a strong emotion in your audience that speaks to their personal ethics or values without going so far as to create a full-on smear campaign against another company. To do this, you need to focus on how you can help the customers.

How to Get Good Press: 5 Steps for Attracting Positive Media Attention

Here are 5 steps for getting good press as a FinTech:

Step 1: Putting Together Your Brand Story

Before you can even begin approaching press and media outlets, you need a very clear brand story that you can communicate to the press and your target audience alike.

A brand story is a narrative tool used in marketing to concisely convey your company's ethics, values, and purpose. Your brand story should be cohesive and inspire a positive and uplifting emotional reaction from your audience.

To create a brand story, you will need to:

- **Describe a Clear Conflict:** When creating a brand story, think about how traditional narrative stories are told. There is often a main hero and a main conflict that hero must face. In your brand story, position the customer in the role of the hero and describe a conflict that they encounter with financial services, such as over-complicated banking processes or inaccessible insurance services. Consider how those conflicts impact their lives on a wider scale, for example, inaccessible financial services could be preventing people from passing referencing checks, thereby making them unable to access suitable housing. This main conflict should be the specific problem your company is capable of solving.

- **Establish Your Brand as a Guide:** If your customer is the hero of this story, then your company is the guide (think Gandalf in *Lord of the Rings* or Mr. Miyagi in the *Karate Kid*). As the guide, it is your responsibility to direct the hero on the correct path to success — in this case, using your products or services to achieve a desired goal.
- **Provide a Compelling Value Proposition:** For your brand story to be effective, you need a powerful value proposition that demonstrates to the customer why you are the perfect company to help them through their story. As part of your value proposition, you should state how you stand apart from competitors.
- **Explain the Stakes of the Situation:** No narrative story is complete without a strong set of high stakes. Think of this as the potential failure if a customer chooses not to work with you — you don't want to scare or threaten the customer, but rather warn them of the struggles they may face without your assistance.
- **Detail How Customers Can Reach Their Goals:** As part of your brand story, provide a clear plan of how the customer can reach their goals with your help. The steps in this plan will form the basis of your narrative, acting as the plot devices that help to move the story forward towards a positive outcome.

Step 2: Approaching PR Companies & Media Outlets

Approaching PR companies and media outlets can be a delicate task, as you want to convince them your company is newsworthy but for good reasons.

To effectively approach PR and media companies, make sure to:

- **Know Your Strengths:** Every FinTech company is likely to have a variety of different channels through which they reach their audience. Knowing which of these are the strongest channels is the key to figuring out who the best PR or media outlets are for reaching out to. For instance, one company may excel at video content on social media, while another may have built an excellent rapport with their local community thanks to their community service efforts.
- **Do Thorough Research:** Always research the PR and media outlets you want to reach out to before actually reaching out. Look for outlets with an audience that includes your target customers and business partners.
- **Develop Compelling Pitches:** When reaching out to a PR or media outlet, chances are you will be requesting that they publish a story about your company. This will require you to write a news story pitch that explains what the story entails and why it is important. At minimum, your pitch should follow a similar outline to your brand story by clearly defining a problem and establishing your company as the guide that can provide the best solution.
- **Keep Timeliness in Mind:** Timeliness refers to how relevant a story is at the current moment. I will discuss timeliness in greater depth in step 5, but keep in mind that FinTech is a highly relevant topic and can be framed as very timely when pitched correctly.

Step 3: Creating a List of Media Contacts

Along with reaching out to PR and media outlets, you should also work on build good working relationships with professionals who work in these fields. Media and PR professionals are often looking for new connections in various industries, including in FinTech — your goal should be to identify these professionals and reach out to them about starting a cooperative relationship. Good types of media professionals to include in your contact list include:

- **General Journalists:** General journalists who report on a wide array of different topics in both technology and finance are always good to have on standby. These types of professionals will often be looking for new and compelling stories to pitch to different outlets and publications.
- **Tech Critics:** When releasing new products or services, it can be helpful to have a tech critic readily available to review your new product and service and report on it to their audience. Just keep in mind that critics can write both positive and negative reviews, so be sure to thoroughly beta test your product before reaching out to a tech critic.
- **Financial Columnists:** Financial columnists are a specific type of journalist that focus primarily on news in the financial industry. With FinTech being a growing sector of the industry, many of these columnists need willing contacts who can provide insights into the latest happenings in FinTech. In exchange, these columnists can feature your company in articles geared toward a highly niche audience.
- **Online Blogs:** These days, online blogs get nearly as much — if not more — web traffic as traditional news and PR outlets. The advantage of online blogs is that they are not bound to specific guidelines that prevent more traditional journalists from writing biased pieces, meaning you are more likely to find a blog that is more willing to write a full feature that positively portrays your company to a large audience.
- **Broadcast & Video Reporters:** Never underestimate the power of video content. Having connections with broadcast journalists, video reporters, and online video content creators is crucial, as these professionals pull some of the largest viewership numbers. Connecting with YouTubers is also a great way to get your name out there.

Step 4: Establishing Yourself as an Industry Authority

When working to achieve good press for your FinTech company, you do not have to rely solely on others to write and publish positive stories about your business.

Having at least one to two staff writers who can pitch stories that they have written to news sites, blogs, and other media outlets helps ensure you always have good press about your company being published.

Plus, having staff writers who can pitch and publish stories will help you to establish yourself as an authority within the FinTech industry. As a result, it will be easier for you to successfully reach out to PR and media companies, as well as build a large media contact list.

Of course, for this approach to be the most effective, your staff writers will also need to be experts in the field of FinTech. As such, you should seek out writers who have:

- **Experience in FinTech:** The best FinTech writers will have at least 1 to 2 years of experience in the industry, either as a writer or in another FinTech role. This experience is essential, as it will make it easier for them to take potentially complex concepts and explain them in a way that is digestible to a wide audience.
- **Knowledge of Trends:** Your writers should not just be experienced in FinTech, they should also be FinTech connoisseurs — passionate professionals with a deep interest in all things FinTech. With a writer that keeps up with all the latest FinTech trends on your side, you can more easily create PR stories that are highly relevant at any given moment.
- **Established Connections:** One of the best advantages to look for in a writer is someone who already has at least a few established connections with PR and media outlets. With an existing positive relationship in place, it will be much easier to convince these outlets of why they should talk about your company and what it has to offer.

Step 5: Being Mindful of Timeliness

One of the most important things to media and PR professionals is timeliness, both in terms of meeting print deadlines and publishing stories that are highly relevant at any given moment.

Timeliness is a term primarily used in journalism that refers to stories that are regarded as newsworthy due to having immediate value and high relevancy to current events. Generally, a timely story will be something that has just happened within the last few days.

This is a critical consideration for FinTech companies looking to attract positive media attention, as media and PR outlets will be the most interested in your story if the main subject of the story is something new that has only been around for a couple of days, such as a new product or service.

If you have a story you want to pitch that doesn't deal with a brand new product or service, then the main topic of the story should be a highly relevant current event to which your product or service is related.

For instance, let's say your company offers a virtual wallet solution that was launched last year. To make this story more timely, you can craft a story about how this virtual wallet can protect users against a new cybersecurity threat that is currently a pressing issue in the industry.

How to Know When You Have a Sellable Story

Typically, a PR or media outlet is not going to be interested in a story that simply talks about you and your company. Your story needs to have a compelling subject outside of just business marketing, such as how your company supported a struggling small business or a successful community event.

According to basic journalism standards, along with timeliness some of the most important factors that make a story notable and newsworthy include:

- **Proximity:** Proximity refers to how localized a story is. For instance, if

your company primarily operates out of the U.S., proximity will often relate to how your product or services affect specific communities within the country. Proximity is most important when dealing with a localized audience, as you will need a story that covers how your product or services can specifically benefit this audience.
- **Impact:** Impact is a journalistic measurement of how consequential a story is and generally covers stories that can change lives. A good example of this is if you offer banking services that are available to unbanked populations, as this can have a tremendous impact on the overall financial accessibility within a community.
- **Novelty:** Novelty is the rare or unusual factor of your story. If you offer a product or service that no other company currently offers, this can be framed as a major innovation that serves as a novelty within a news story.
- **Conflict:** As we have covered, conflict is an important part of any story. If there has been a recent conflict in the FinTech industry, sharing your company's opinion and insights — as well as how your company can help solve this conflict — can be very impactful.
- **Human Interest:** Human interest stories are those that tug at our heartstrings, especially when it comes to companies taking the time to perform charitable community outreach and uplift their local business communities.
- **Prominence:** A prominent news story involves a prominent public figure. In the case of FinTech, this can include major financial and technology leaders.

Ideally, for your story to be both effective and compelling to PR and media outlets, it should contain at least 3 of these factors — with timeliness being one of the most important.

Newsletters

You've got mail!

Why Start a Newsletter?

If you have ever looked into email marketing, you have undoubtedly come across a million and one websites, articles, and books telling you to start a newsletter.

Well, make it one million and two, because a newsletter is one of the best marketing tactics of the modern age. In the B2B Content Marketing 2020 research report, it was uncovered that 81% of B2B marketers use email newsletters as a main form of content.

Furthermore, a 2021 Hubspot survey of more than 1,000 B2B and B2C customers around the globe found that 35% of marketers' companies leverage email as a marketing channel, with only social media (44%) and websites and blogs (36%) topping it.

But why is email marketing and, more specifically, publishing a newsletter so impactful?

For starters, there are many different purposes a newsletter can serve, including:

- **Weekly/Monthly Updates:** One of the more common uses for a newsletter is to share weekly or monthly updates with your subscribers. This is particularly useful for companies who maintain and regularly post to a website blog, as the newsletter can be a good method for directing readers

to new posts. Moreover, update newsletters offer the right opportunity to promote any sales or discounts you have running at the moment.
- **Welcome Series:** Whenever someone new signs up for your newsletter subscription list, it is important to nurture this lead and ensure you categorize them correctly for your audience segmentation. Your welcome series can help your reader get to know you better and allow you the opportunity to learn more about your potential customer or business partner as well.
- **Employee Spotlights:** Here you can show off your team. This helps establish credibility and trust among your clients, as knowing who you are working with adds a human touch that many customers are searching for from financial services companies. Employee spotlights are a great way to highlight your team's strengths while also rewarding them for their hard work.
- **Special Announcements:** Whether you are releasing a new product, updating a service, doing a rebrand, or anything else, a newsletter is the perfect place for announcing it to your valued clients. Chances are good that the people subscribed to your newsletter include your most dedicated customers, so using a newsletter to reach these customers with special announcements first is an excellent way to further solidify that loyalty.
- **Loyalty Programs:** Along with sending special announcement messages to your customers, a newsletter can also be a good way to run a loyalty program. For instance, you could create a segment within your email marketing system to send loyalty rewards to returning customers who have subscribed for a specific length of time. Loyalty program newsletters may contain special deals, personalized messages, or other elements that set them apart from the standard newsletter.

Three benefits of publishing a newsletter include:

- **Boosted Brand Recognition:** Even to this day, email is one of the most used forms of communication.
- **Increased Conversions:** Newsletters are a great way to nurture leads who

may not be ready to make a purchase or sign a business deal just yet. A newsletter can serve as a reminder to your potential customers of all that you have to offer and that you would love to do business with them.
- **Improved Customer Relations:** A newsletter can also help your customers feel as though they are more connected to you and that it is easy to stay in touch with you. This can improve the overall impression your clients have of your company.

How to Start a Newsletter

Step 1: Determine the Tone & Theme of Your Newsletter

So, you're starting to write your first newsletter — but what is it about?

Do you want a newsletter that has many subscribers thanks to the frequent deals it offers? How about a newsletter that is well-loved by its subscribers for the compelling insights it shares?

Determining the purpose of your newsletter and consider your desired tone and theme.

For example, picture a FinTech company that specializes in cloud migrations.

This company may choose to write a newsletter all about the cloud, providing useful tips for getting more out of the cloud and educational resources for customers who may be unfamiliar with this technology.

With this cloud-themed newsletter, the company might send out a regular monthly series covering a specific topic about the cloud, such as how the cloud works or how to store your data on the cloud. The tone of this newsletter is educational and resourceful, serving as a guide for customers new to the cloud.

At the end of the newsletter, the company may choose to include a call to action or company update — this, however, should be kept brief.

Step 2: Set Clear Expectations for Your Newsletter

As you start gathering emails for your newsletter subscription list, it is important to consider how you will introduce the first newsletter to these readers.

In your initial welcome newsletter, set clear expectations for what readers will get out of being subscribed. Alternatively, you can set up a formal landing page for your newsletter that readers can visit to learn all about what to expect from a subscription.

Key expectations to set include:

- **Sending Frequency:** Tell people how often they will receive your newsletter, and stick to your word. If you say you will send one newsletter twice per week, maintaining this schedule is crucial for establishing consistency and trust.
- **Topic & Theme:** Let your readers know what kind of content they will receive through your newsletter subscription. Whether this is educational articles, how-to guides, product reviews, or anything else, make it clear what the overarching theme of your newsletter is and offer examples of the kinds of content you will publish.
- **Subscription Instructions:** You never want to make your clients feel like you are forcing them to read your newsletter. Offer clear instructions on how to pause, cancel, or mute a newsletter subscription.
- **Loyalty Rewards:** If you plan on incorporating a loyalty program into your newsletter, communicate this to your readers. This should inform them of how often to expect rewards and some examples of what those rewards may be (i.e. a free month of a specific service or 5 free GB of cloud-based storage.
- **Feedback:** Most importantly, tell your readers how they can give you feedback. Reader feedback is one of the best ways to improve your newsletter's effectiveness, alongside tracking key performance metrics such as click rates and conversions.

In addition to setting these expectations clearly and plainly for your readers, you should also make it explicitly clear when someone is about to subscribe to your newsletter.

A newsletter is only at its most effective when the people reading it are genuinely interested and want to learn more. Tricking people into signing up for your newsletter may result in higher initial subscriptions but will do nothing to help you retain those subscribers long-term, and is possibly illegal depending on where your subscribers are based.

Step 3: Make Unsubscribing Simple

Here's the golden rule: **make it ridiculously easy to unsubscribe from your newsletter**.

For many people, too many emails coming in too frequently can feel more like a hassle than a benefit. If these people want to unsubscribe from your newsletter to help clean up their inboxes, make it clear how they can do that.

By making it difficult to unsubscribe from your newsletter, all you are ultimately accomplishing is a bad impression of your business and an unsatisfied reader.

Moreover, there are email-focused regulations that exists in various regions around the world which you'll need to familiarize yourself with to ensure you are complying with local and national laws.

For example, in the U.S., the CAN-SPAM Act requires businesses to tell recipients how to opt-out of receiving emails from you in the future and to honor these opt-outs immediately, among other things. Back on this side of the pond, the European Union has the Directive on Privacy and Electronic Communications, and several individual European countries have their own separate regulations as well.

Two good online resources for learning more about regional anti-spam and email laws are Licks Attorney's Compliance Blog and Vertical Response.

Step 4: Create a Lead Magnet

A lead magnet is a branded item or piece of content that is given away to people for free in exchange for their contact information — namely, their email address.

When promoting a lead magnet, it is important to make it clear that in order to receive the product, you must first sign up for the newsletter.

Lead magnets can come in many forms, including:

- Ebooks
- Webinars
- Templates
- Training Videos
- How-To Guides

No matter what type of content you choose as your lead magnet, your lead magnet must still stand on its own as an informative and beneficial resource.

Step 5: Set Up Your Newsletter

We have arrived at, arguably, the most time-consuming step in this entire process — it's time to set up your first official newsletter.

In terms of the structure of your newsletter, there are 5 structural elements:

1. **The Subject Line:** Since most newsletters are delivered to customers via email, considering what to say in your email subject line is vital. The subject line should pique your reader's interest, compelling them to open the email and read your newsletter. Avoid over-complicating this, you only have a few seconds to get someone's attention, you don't want to lose it.
2. **The Header:** The header is the top of the actual newsletter, and is contained within an email. Key components to include in a header include a visually pleasing banner image, the brand and/or name of your

company, and the title of your newsletter. Your newsletter title can be the same as your subject line in some cases. Again, the simpler, the better.
3. **The Section Headlines:** Most newsletters will contain more than one article of information, often offering a short summary of a longer written post or product description, as well as a link to the full story or product webpage. Above these short summaries should be headlines that clearly list what information or details each section contains.
4. **The Body Text:** The body text of a newsletter is the meatiest part of your newsletter, letting the reader know about any news, upcoming events, deals, and more that you may have to share. A newsletter's body text should captivate the audience fully and make them feel invested in whatever story you are telling, whether that's a recent business development or a major upcoming product update.
5. **The Call to Action:** Finally, to achieve a successful newsletter structure, you need a strong call to action (CTA). It is always a good idea to list CTAs both above and below the fold (the fold being the area of a newsletter at which point the reader has to scroll to continue reading).

How to Use Newsletter & Email Software

Once you have your base newsletter structure squared away, your next step is to set up the newsletter software of your choosing.

This setup process can vary drastically depending on what website-building platform or tools you used. I'll start with how to set up two of the most popular email marketing software options — MailChimp and Sendinblue — on a WordPress site.

To set up a MailChimp newsletter subscription feature on your WordPress website, follow these steps:

- Generate an API Key in MailChimp to connect the WordPress plugin to.
- Go to the WordPress Plugins marketplace and select MailChimp List Subscribe Form, then select download to begin installing.

Installation for Version 2.8+:

- First, you must unzip the archive and upload the MailChimp directory to your /wp-content/plugins/directory
- Next, activate the plugin in the Plugins menu in WordPress
- Navigate to "Settings" and select "MailChimp Setup"
- Enter and verify your MailChimp API Key

Installation for Custom Code:

- To add the plugin to a php code block, enter:

mailchimpSF_signup_form();

- To add the plugin in between HTML, enter

<?php mailchimpSF_signup_form(); ?>

To set up a Sendinblue newsletter subscription feature on your WordPress website, follow these steps:

- Create a Sendinblue account and find your API key
- Log in as an admin to your WordPress dashboard and go to "Plugins"
- Select "Add New" and search for Sendinblue — the name of the plugin is "Newsletter, SMTP, Email marketing, and Subscribe forms by Sendinblue"
- Select "Install Now" for this plugin and then "Activate"
- Once the Sendinblue tab appears on your WordPress sidebar menu, click on it
- Enter your API key into the plugin and click "Login"

If you created your website using a website-building platform like Wix or Squarespace, these platforms have their own built-in newsletter features and tools. Depending on which platform you are using, you will likely easily be able to integrate a MailChimp or Sendinblue add-in to your site as you would on WordPress.

If you worked with a developer (or if you are a developer) to create your website, your best option is to ask another developer (or the same one if you are still in contact) to add a newsletter subscription feature and landing page.

How to Send Readers Through the Correct Funnels

If you choose MailChimp as your software for creating and sending out a newsletter, you can take advantage of their advanced marketing funnel features.

I spoke about marketing funnels in an earlier chapter, and they're an important part of newsletters. With newsletters, by creating different funnels or segments, you can separate customers into various groups based on their similarities and how close they are to purchasing.

For example, you can set up a funnel to send a special welcome edition of your newsletter to new subscribers. This funnel may include a series of welcome emails that help to build the subscriber's awareness of your brand and what you have to offer.

Comparatively, for long-term subscribers who you are trying to nurture, you can set up a funnel that sends these subscribers newsletters with special deals or discounts to encourage them to take action.

On MailChimp, the marketing funnel tools for an email newsletter come in the form of Audience Segmentation.

Here's how to set up audience segmentation on MailChimp:

- Before beginning the segmentation process, you should first review MailChimp's pre-built segments available through the free version and the advanced segments available through the premium version. This will help you decide which version you require.
- Once you know what type of account you need with MailChimp, create a segment from your contact table.

To create a complex segment:

- Select either contacts match "all" or "any" of the following conditions — any means the person only has to meet one of the conditions you have set, all means they must meet all of the conditions.
- Select "Audience" and then "Segments"
- Select "Create Segment"
- Set your first condition in the drop-down menu and select "Add" to create the next condition
- Preview the Segment and edit as needed
- Save the Segment

To create a simple segment:

- Select "Audience" and then "Segments"
- Select "Create Segment" or select any current audience segments you have to edit them
- View the drop-down menus and set them to "Date Added", "is after", and "the last campaign was sent"
- Preview the Segment
- Save the Segment
- Create your targeted newsletters for each segment. When you are ready to send them, you can start from either the Segments page or the campaign builder.

Step 6: Stick to a Consistent & Unobtrusive Schedule

As mentioned earlier, consistency is a priority when publishing a newsletter.

Your readers need to have a clear expectation of when your newsletter will arrive in their inbox. On the other hand, you must allow your readers the opportunity to set expectations for you as well regarding how often they are comfortable with receiving email correspondence.

The trick with email marketing is that it is less about bombarding your subscribers with content every single day and more about creating consistent, high-quality content that provides real value.

In turn, this value you are providing to your readers slowly turns into brand loyalty, leading many to switch from bystanders to active customers at your business.

If you are unsure if your publishing schedule is too frequent or intrusive, you can ask your readers for feedback. To increase your chances of receiving feedback responses, offer a special deal or free item in exchange for the reader's thoughts and opinions.

Step 7: Maintain a Personal Touch

A common issue that potential customers have with email marketing campaigns is that they feel too obviously automated. The lack of a personal, human touch can really take away from a reader's overall experience with your newsletter and ultimately lead them to unsubscribe.

Here are 4 tips for maintaining a personal touch in your newsletter as you scale:

- **Use Your Professional Email:** Rather than using a generic email like hello@yourcompany.com as the sender, your newsletter should be sent directly from you. Having your name (or the name of a marketing team member) in the email address makes your newsletter feel more like a personalized letter from a friend.
- **Personalize Greetings & Sign-Offs:** Email marketing tools often offer features that can automatically add a personalized greeting and sign-off to your emails, including your newsletters. A personalized greeting addresses a recipient by name, while a sign-off gives the conclusion to your newsletter a more human-like touch.
- **Incorporate Interactive Elements:** To help your readers feel involved in the newsletter, include interactive elements, such as polls or links to surveys. Not only does this give your readers a sense of inclusion and participation but it also gives you the opportunity to learn more about

your potential customers' preferences and spending habits.
- **Keep Your Design Simple:** Sometimes, the simplest designs are the best designs. We're so used to seeing stereotypical newsletter emails in our inboxes that we tend to ignore them. A newsletter that is very simple in its design, sort of like a news article in your inbox, can get better results and more concisely convey a message to your readers.

Step 8: Build & Nurture Your Email List

As mentioned, lead magnets are one of the most effective ways to get people to sign up for your newsletter subscription list. Once you have a strong foundation of subscribers, however, it's up to you to figure out how you are going to keep them.

This is where nurturing comes in.

To create a successful email nurture campaign with your newsletter, you should:

- **Develop a Deep Understanding of the Reader:** To truly nurture a lead via email, you need a clear understanding of their personality, lifestyle, and behaviors to create a nurture sequence that works for them. As you build your email list, using your newsletter to gain more information and feedback from readers is crucial to sending more personalized and effective emails.
- **Segment Your Audience Further:** Once you have divided your audience into a few main segments, you can segment these groups even further according to their specific email habits and digital behavior (which can be tracked via analytical tools). By segmenting your audience in this way, you can make your newsletters and emails all the more personalized.
- **Plan Separate Sequences for Each Segment:** While you may have one main newsletter that everyone on your email list receives, it can be useful to plan out newsletter-like sequences to send to your individual audience segments. These newsletters should vary in content to more accurately match the needs and wants of the segment they are sent to.

- **Measure Your Success with Analytics:** Using an email marketing platform like MailChimp allows you access to analytics that help you track the performance of your newsletter and email marketing efforts.
- **Set Sequence Triggers:** Rather than planning an email sequence according to a set schedule, you can instead set automated sequence triggers that send an email after a specific condition is met. For instance, you could set a sequence trigger for when someone makes a purchase and have the corresponding email be a how-to guide for how to use the product or service the customer just purchased.

All in all, what's most important is to always make your newsletters and other email marketing sequences a thing of true value to your customers. When your customers walk away from a newsletter feeling more informed, educated, and valued, that's a fundamentally important step to building a long-lasting clientele.

Thank You

Thank you so much for reading. It honestly means the world to me that you reached the end! If you want to get in touch with me, you can find me on:
   Email at deborah@fintechcontentmarketing.com
   LinkedIn at Deborah Boyland
   My website at fintechcontentmarketing.com
   IG @themightydebatha

I've love to hear your thoughts, if there was anything you disagreed with, or anything that helped you and your team.

If you could leave a review, that would also be amazing, it doesn't have to be good, or particularly kind, any feedback that could help future readers decide if this is the right book for them would be a huge help.

Thanks again,
   Deborah x

References

https://support.google.com/google-ads/answer/1704371?hl=en#:~:text=The%20cost%20for%20each%20keyword,customer%20might%20be%20searching%20for.

https://blog.hootsuite.com/instagram-demographics/#Instagram_age_demographics

https://wallaroomedia.com/blog/social-media/tiktok-statistics/#:~:text=U.S.%20Audience%20%E2%80%93%20As%20we%20mentioned,between%20the%20ages%2025%2D44.

https://blog.hootsuite.com/twitter-demographics/#:~:text=Most%20Twitter%20users%20are%20between,is%20probably%20for%20the%20best.

https://influencermarketinghub.com/pinterest-stats/#:~:text=A%20survey%20of%20Pinterest%20users,Gen%20Z%20users%20in%202021.

https://blog.hootsuite.com/linkedin-demographics-for-business/#age

https://www.insiderintelligence.com/content/facebook-still-accounts-quarter-of-us-digital-ad-spending

https://www.insiderintelligence.com/insights/facebook-advertising-statistics/

https://www.facebook.com/business/industries/financial-services

https://www.smartinsights.com/digital-marketing-strategy/financial-services-social-media-strategy-trends-and-recommendations/

https://www.linkedin.com/business/marketing/blog/trends-tips/emarketers-b2b-advertising-forecast-2021-6-key-insights-and-revelations

https://www.insiderintelligence.com/content/digital-trust-benchmark-report-2021

https://www.businessofapps.com/data/tik-tok-statistics/

https://www.technologyreview.com/2022/07/14/1055935/making-the-inv

isible-visible-doing-more-with-data/

https://www.cnbc.com/2022/06/08/stripe-co-founder-defends-company-against-unfair-competition-claims.html

https://blog.hubspot.com/blog/tabid/6307/bid/7007/how-a-block-of-ice-increased-one-company-s-customers-by-225.aspx

https://contentmarketinginstitute.com/wp-content/uploads/2019/10/2020_B2B_Research_Final.pdf

https://blog.hubspot.com/marketing/hubspot-blog-marketing-industry-trends-report?_ga=2.125310921.2116605659.1655405116-782004359.1655405116

https://www.lickslegal.com/post/anti-spam-laws-around-the-world#:~:text=Once%20people%20say%20they%20don,with%20the%20CAN%2DSPAM%20Act.

https://verticalresponse.com/blog/email-anti-spam-laws-around-the-world-infographic/

www.ingramcontent.com/pod-product-compliance
Lightning Source LLC
Chambersburg PA
CBHW050004230526
45465CB00003BB/1260